HOLLYWOOD
MONSTER

HOLLYWOOD MONSTER

A WALK DOWN ELM STREET WITH
THE MAN OF YOUR DREAMS

ROBERT ENGLUND

WITH ALAN GOLDSHER

WITH INTRODUCTIONS BY
WES CRAVEN AND TOBE HOOPER

POCKET BOOKS
New York   London   Toronto   Sydney

Pocket Books
A Division of Simon & Schuster, Inc.
1230 Avenue of the Americas
New York, NY 10020

First Pocket Books hardcover edition October 2009

POCKET and colophon are registered trademarks of Simon & Schuster, Inc.

For information about special discounts for bulk purchases, please contact Simon & Schuster Special Sales at 1-866-506-1949 or business@simonandschuster.com

The Simon & Schuster Speakers Bureau can bring authors to your live event. For more information or to book an event contact the Simon & Schuster Speakers Bureau at 1-866-248-3049 or visit our website at www.simonspeakers.com.

Designed by Renata Di Biase

Manufactured in the United States of America

10 9 8 7 6 5 4 3 2 1

Library of Congress Cataloging-in-Publication Data

Englund, Robert
  Hollywood monster : a walk down Elm Street with the man of your dreams / Robert Englund with Alan Goldsher ; with introductions by Wes Craven and Tobe Hooper.
    p. cm.
  1. Englund, Robert. 2. Actors—United States—Biography. I. Title.
PN2287.E545A3 2009
791.4302'8092—dc22
  [B]   2009026576

ISBN 978-1-4391-5049-8

HOLLYWOOD
MONSTER

INTRODUCTION
BY WES CRAVEN

I FIRST MET ROBERT ENGLUND WHILE CASTING for the actor to play my archvillain, Freddy Krueger, in *A Nightmare on Elm Street*. At that time, I didn't know exactly what Freddy would look like, or sound like, or even act like. I just knew I wanted him to be evil, and smart. The devil's not stupid. That's what makes him scary.

I was leaning toward finding someone old. An old, evil man who delighted in the torment of children—reveled in the destruction of innocence itself. And he needed to be physically intimidating, of course.

So I was looking at old stuntmen.

It wasn't working out well. I was discovering that stuntmen were not particularly drawn to being cruel, nor did they get enthusiastic about taking delight in murdering children. Same for older men. They, like the stuntmen, had seen a lot of life, knew how fragile it was, and just couldn't put themselves into such a state of mind. Too uncomfortable.

Then in walked Robert.

I'D SEEN HIM IN his role of Willie, the friendly alien in the television movie *V*, and in the subsequent miniseries of the same name. A nice, sympathetic alien, with twinkling eyes and an earnest, almost shy personality. And Robert pretty much looked like that. Friendly, chatty, brimming with humor and energy. *That's not Freddy Krueger,* I told myself inwardly. *He's too nice. And young.*

But what overwhelmed my doubts was Robert's enthusiasm for the role, his unabashed eagerness to play someone really evil. He saw the role, and the script as a whole, pretty much as I saw it, as some kind of black comedy, and as the telling of a story about iconic figures locked in the eternal human struggle between good and evil—a modern myth, disguised as a scare-the-pants-off-you horror movie. Robert got it.

And he got the role.

WHAT FOLLOWED WAS PURE pleasure on my part, and pure hard work on Robert's. For openers, Freddy wasn't a man without dermatological problems. In his past incarnation, while still on earth, he'd been burned alive by the equivalent of a lynch mob and was horribly scarred. The mask of scar tissue would give him both the power of the typically masked villain—such as Jason, and Michael Myers, and a multitude of others—but it would also allow him the freedom of expression that a rigid mask would not. Unfortunately for Robert, that meant three hours in the makeup chair every morning before he even got a chance to act. And the stuff stayed on all day. Try eating lunch through latex sometime. It's not pleasant.

But once he was on camera, Robert Englund disappeared, and this strange, powerful, wickedly funny, and terrifyingly dangerous man emerged: Freddy Krueger. And from that moment on until the makeup was pulled off at day's end, Freddy ruled the set. Into the basic character I'd invented, Robert poured a host of improvisations—wisecracks and scary stances and poses, and a chilling sort of creeping walk that just made your blood run cold.

It was astonishing to watch, and I knew right away that the picture and the villain that brought it to life were going to be classics.

BUT ROBERT HAD ANOTHER surprising side as well: the gentle, affable, and patient star—and that's what he quickly became, a star—a man who liked kids and didn't mind signing endless autographs, or doing other things that took him far out of his way, just to spread happiness their way. I'll tell you a story.

Once a psychiatrist wrote me. He had a young patient who had heard of Freddy Krueger and was having nightmares about him. I really wanted to help, so I got in touch with Robert and asked if he would say a few words to the kid into a vidcam. Not only did Robert do that, but he did it while he was being put into, and then out of, his Freddy makeup, describing each step of the way how Freddy was nothing more than latex and glue, and nothing to be worried about.

Shortly after I mailed the tape to the doctor, I received a

letter in return. The youngster was not only cured, he wanted to watch a Freddy movie!

Over the years I've spent many hours with Robert, especially in foreign cities for film festivals, and have constantly marveled at the scope of his celebrity. He's recognized everywhere, and the huge grins that spread across people's faces when they see him are priceless. Robert Englund is one of those rare walking contradictions: scary as heck when he's working; and delightful, witty, and erudite when he's not—and he always makes time for the fans who are eager to shake his hand.

So long as he does it without the glove.

INTRODUCTION
BY TOBE HOOPER

*I*N 1974, NOT TOO LONG AFTER I SHOT *THE Texas Chain Saw Massacre,* I was checking out a movie at an art theater—at least that's what they called 'em around Austin, Texas, college campuses, art theaters; I don't know what they called 'em in New York or wherever—called *Buster and Billie.* It starred some hot guy and a good-looking girl, and they were great, but there was this little albino costar, a high-powered fireball of mischief and energy. I watched this man smoke up the screen and thought, *Who the hell is this? The energy that he has, the passion, the verisimilitude, the chops, man, this cat is great!*

That was the first time I ever saw Robert Englund. And, man, I hoped it wouldn't be the last.

A COUPLE YEARS LATER, I was in a casting session for a movie I was directing called *Eaten Alive.* I was wrapping up a rambling conversation with the great character actor Neville Brand, during which time he convinced me that he should play the lead, when in walked Robert, and I thought, *Farrrrrrr out. It's that guy. It's the albino from that art movie. It's Robert fucking Englund.* After Neville took off, I told Robert, "Man,

I'm a big fan of yours. But I'm also becoming a big fan of the casting director who sent me you and Neville." Robert read a few lines from the script, then we talked about *Buster and Billie,* and we vibed, so there wasn't any of that Let-Me-See-Other-People-And-I'll-Get-Back-To-You bullshit. I didn't need to waste his time. I didn't need to waste my breath. He had the part before he left the room.

The thing about Robert as an actor is, he'll always offer you eight hundred different choices for each scene, but even if you agree on something Tuesday night, he'll come to work on Wednesday morning with eight hundred more ideas. He's so in the moment, and when the space or atmosphere changes, Robert changes right with it, and that makes for great filmmaking.

ROBERT WAS A DELIGHT to work with from the first second, unbelievably inventive, as much of a fireball as I could've hoped for. But as energetic as he was, his subtlety was what consistently blew me away. In one scene—and this was a tiny moment, but it's these sorts of tiny moments that turn a movie into art—he shuffled his feet and kicked some dust up onto Neville's pants, as if he were a dog who'd just taken a piss and wanted to cover it up. Only about three seconds of screen time, but it was the most unique fucking thing I'd ever seen, and the best part about Robert is that he brings all kinds of unique fucking things to each of his characters. Now I like unique fucking things, so Robert and I became fast friends.

We're both movie guys, and this was a moment in time when film could rightly be called art, so we always had plenty to talk about, and our discussions were a lot farther out and cooler than your typical movie-set conversation. I suspect that people would've been surprised had they known that Mr. Chainsaw Massacre and Freddy Krueger spent an inordinate amount of time chatting about Greek mythology and Fellini.

Twenty years after *Eaten Alive*—that's twenty fucking years, dear readers—I brought my old friend aboard to star in *The Mangler*, a movie that in spite of a grueling shoot in South Africa ended up being one of my favorites.

Robert's character, Bill Gartley, walked with crutches and leg braces, and even though he had to hobble around the set for eighteen hours a day, Robert wasn't at all fazed, even when he had to do his own stunts. In one scene, Robert was supposed to get hit with a lamp, then do a cartwheel and end up out of frame. To allow him to really go for it, we had a couple of people standing off to the side, ready to catch him, because if he'd have fallen at the speed he was moving, he'd have been dead. After we shot the stunt a couple of times, I watched it in my monitor, trying to decide whether I wanted to try it again. I was all lost in my head when I heard a puppy dog whimpering over my left shoulder. I turned around, and there's Robert. "I think my wig is fucked," he said. "I think my makeup is fucked. And to make things even worse, when they caught me after my cartwheel, they put me on the concrete floor, and this big Teamster stepped on my head." He pointed at his face. "And look at this." One of his eyes was hanging from its socket, and the other was gushing tears. Now, the eye hanging from the socket was fake, of course, but it was still stunning, and all I could do was laugh. That movie was a bitch to make—we accidentally spilled a shitload of fake blood, and one of our key grips was electrocuted on three separate occasions—and if Robert hadn't graciously hauled ten-some-odd cartons of Marlboros with him from the States, I don't know if I would've been able to make it through the film with my sanity intact.

IN THE HORROR PANTHEON, there's Frankenstein, there's Dracula, there's Michael Myers, there's my main man Leatherface, and there's Freddy Krueger. Freddy's right up there in the Fucked-Up Shit Hall of Fame, and that's almost all Robert. Most of these other literal and figurative monsters are completely hidden and unrecognizable under a mask, but Robert's right out there for the world to see, oozing blisters and all. This is a small batch of people we're talking about here, dear readers: Boris Karloff, Bela Lugosi, Lon Chaney, and Robert Englund—and I'm honored that this fireball graced my film sets. And I can't wait to work with him again, so I can deposit more Robert Englund memories in my memory bank.

CHAPTER 1

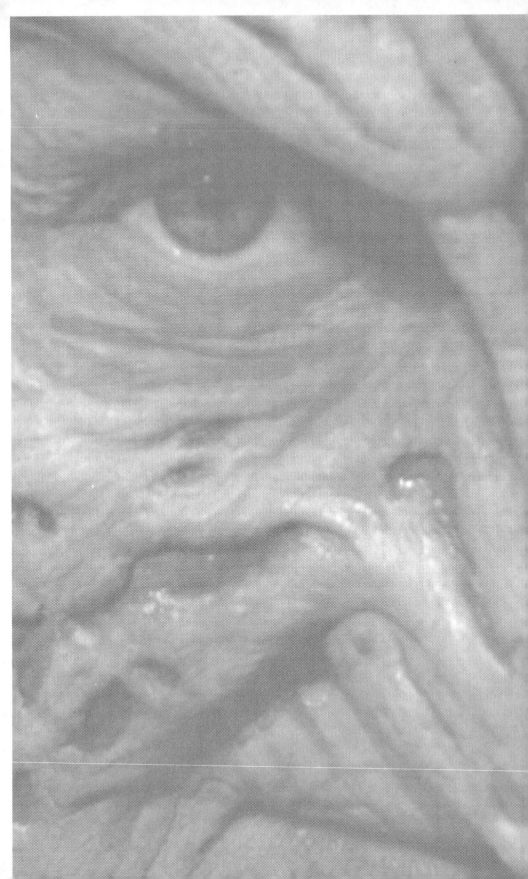

NIGHTMARE #1:

Zanita MacMillan was the most beautiful girl in the sixth grade. Like most of the other boys on the playground, I had a crush on her. Zanita would visit me in my dreams and my preadolescent fantasies. Eventually she showed up as the heroine in my recurring Cold War nightmare. The nightmare always ended with my head cradled in Zanita's lap, a thin trickle of blood at the corner of my mouth, and hordes of North Korean Communists replete with long winter jackets, combat boots, and army-issue hats, earflaps up, emblazoned with a single red star in the center, overrunning the playground. In the nightmare, I had fought to the end and was wounded and dying. The enemy soldiers swarmed over the school fences, commandeered the elementary school rooftops, and slowly advanced on Zanita and me as we huddled against the handball court. This was either the product of too many war movies or too many drop-and-cover drills. It recurred for years. And years. And years.

S TEPHANIE WAS THE BELLE OF THE BALL, THE most popular girl in my junior high school. She was pretty, and sweet, and I had a tiny bit of a crush on her, so when I found out she was involved with a semiprofessional children's theater in the San Fernando Valley called the Teenage Drama Workshop, I was intrigued. If acting was cool to the cutest eighth-grade girl in the Valley, that was good enough for me, so when she invited me to check out a show, I couldn't refuse.

Turned out this Teenage Drama Workshop was a big deal, more than just some rinky-dink community theater, and featured child actors from all over the country, some of whom ultimately became professionals. The first time I went to see Stephanie perform, for instance, I was struck dumb by her young, brunette costar, Sharon Hugueny. Sharon, who, come the early 1960s, became a teen heartthrob and appeared in films and on television with the likes of Troy Donahue, Sandra Dee, and Peter Fonda, was a knockout, and I was smitten. If I could meet girls like Stephanie and Sharon while hanging around this theater workshop, well, the stage sounded like the place to be.

The following summer, I offered the Workshop my services, such as they were; having never acted before, I figured I'd start out at the bottom of the totem pole, maybe work as an usher, or a behind-the-scenes, backstage helper. Although they didn't need me to do the grunt work, they did let me audition. As it turned out, I landed most of the male leads. I'd never taken a single acting class, and there I was, in the Valley, fronting an entire cast, getting boiled as Hansel in *Hansel and Gretel*, and experiencing for the first time the application of special effects makeup as Pinocchio. (Who knew this would be the first of thousands of makeup sessions I would endure over the years?) However, Pinocchio's elongated nose was far easier to apply, not to mention it was infinitely less itchy than Freddy Krueger's prolonged makeup process.

I went to the Workshop hoping to meet girls, and despite having zero stage experience, I won role after role after role. But I shouldn't have been surprised that I took to it so quickly. Where I grew up, movies and movie people were everywhere; we'd even see Clark Gable in the local grocery store. As a kid I stood transfixed, watching cowboy stuntmen do horse falls on the RKO backlot behind my house. My uncles were television editors and allowed me to visit the sets of the hit shows they were working on. It was, as they say, in my blood.

MY MOM AND DAD weren't stage parents by any means; they themselves had nothing to do with the film industry. My father, Kent, was an executive at Lockheed Aircraft; it wasn't the most glamorous job in California, but he loved it. Before Lockheed, my father had worked for Hughes Aircraft. One morning, well before the sun had even risen, Dad went to work at Burbank Airfield. One of the hangar doors was wide-open, and parked in front of the hangar was a luxurious roadster. The car door had been left open, so Dad glanced in and was treated to a view of a gorgeous woman in a cocktail dress, curled up in the back, happily snoring away. Nonplussed, he walked into the hangar and there was Howard Hughes, one of the richest men in the world, sitting in the cockpit of one of his planes messing around with the wing-flap controls, a goofy smile plastered on his face, looking like a little kid playing with a new toy. (Personally, if I were Howard, I'd have been more interested in messing around with the girl in the limo, but that's just me.)

My mother, Janis, was a stay-at-home mom, but she'd previously led quite the adventurous life. She met Dad in Rio de Janeiro during World War II while they were both teaching the Brazilian air force how to fly their new aircraft. Mom grew up in the same neighborhood with the Little Rascals and King Kong's girlfriend, Fay Wray, and roomed with future film starlets in college. She wasn't in the movie industry, but she was definitely surrounded by it.

Mom loved good books, Dad loved jazz, and they both loved going to the movies, exploring the California coast, and making yearly trips to Santa Fe, New Mexico. Every other week, the movie theater near our house in Encino ran preview screenings of upcoming films, so twice a month Mom and Dad took me to see the latest and greatest movies that Hollywood had to offer, some of which became classics (e.g., *On the Waterfront, Guns of Navarone*, and *Anatomy of a Murder*), and some of which didn't (e.g., I don't remember the titles, because, well, they were stinkers). My parents would drag me along whether or not the content was "appropriate" for little Robbie Englund—some of this grown-up fare intrigued, frightened, or confused the shit out of me, frankly, which undoubtedly played a role in my eventual appreciation for dark material.

Some might say I fell for acting so hard because I'm an only child, and only children crave constant attention, and what better way to get noticed than on the stage or the screen. Having known my fair share of actors who don't have siblings, I can agree that, yes, some of these people are spoiled attention-seekers; however, I've met just as many kids socially damaged by the popularity of an older brother or sister.

We had a happy home, and I was always surrounded by friends and family, always busy, always sleeping over at somebody's house, always encouraged to take advantage of everything life had to offer, always loved. (If Freddy Krueger had been brought up like me, there wouldn't have been any nightmares on Elm Street.) My family's only major issue was that for a few years before his retirement, Dad tended to work too many hours, and my mother got lonely and downed a few too many martinis; it was a *very* minor-league version of *Revolutionary Road*. Considering the kind of crap I saw happening to some of our family's friends, I couldn't complain.

MY YOUNG LIFE WAS good, but it improved dramatically when I suddenly acquired an older sister. Okay, she wasn't *exactly* a sister, but I claimed her as my own.

I was almost thirteen when my parents' goddaughter Gail's parents passed away; good godparents that they were, Mom and Dad insisted Gail come and live with us. There was understandably a palpable sense of sadness when she moved in, but as badly as I felt for Gail, I was thrilled to have her around. Gail was lovely, poised, and graceful, and even a finalist in the Miss California pageant. She treated me like a little brother and actually enjoyed it when I tagged along with her on her adventures.

One night each week, Gail taught swimming classes at the Beverly Hills High School indoor swimming pool, the same one that opens beneath Jimmy Stewart's feet in *It's a Wonderful Life*, and she used to take me along with her in her Chevrolet convertible. After class, we'd go to a drive-in restaurant and have hamburgers and shakes. There I was, in a canary yellow Chevy, sitting next to my beautiful semi-sister, feeling like I was just about the coolest thirteen-year-old in Los Angeles. (All that said, sometimes being in such close proximity to Gail was a bit of a challenge. Her bedroom was right next to mine, and when she'd come out of the shower wearing one of her silky baby-doll nightgowns, things got a little intense for a certain hormone-raging adolescent.)

Some nights after swim class, Gail would let me come over to her boyfriend's apartment, where the two of them would abandon me on the couch in front of the TV. These were vital formative moments for me, not because I overheard my pseudo-sister fooling around with her baseball-player, beatnik boyfriend, but rather because I was introduced to the world of late-night TV talk shows. I discovered Jack Paar, Lenny Bruce, Johnny Carson, and Don Rickles, but my late-night idol was

Steve Allen . . . whom I had the good fortune to meet . . . and who, it turned out, kinda liked me.

One of Steve's friend's daughters was a member of the ensemble in that infamous Teenage Drama Workshop production of *Pinocchio*. After our highly successful opening-night performance, Mr. Allen came backstage to pay his respects. Naturally most everybody in the cast and crew surrounded him, peppering the poor guy with questions and autograph requests. He good-naturedly schmoozed with everybody, then eventually called out, "Okay, where's Pinocchio?"

I shyly raised my hand. "Over here."

He said, "Come with me," then took me by the elbow, pulled me back behind the scenery, and said, "Listen, fella, you're funny as hell. You're special. Keep it up."

I stared at his slicked-back hair and those big glasses and mumbled a thank-you, realizing how amazing it was to get professional approval from somebody as accomplished as Steve Allen. That sort of thing doesn't happen anymore. I'm not seeing David Letterman wander backstage at a junior high production of *You're a Good Man, Charlie Brown*, seek out the kid who played Linus, and tell him he's doing great work. Steve Allen said I was special, but in fact *he* was the special one.

I must've been doing something right during *Pinocchio* because Steve Allen wasn't the only guy who singled me out for notice. Each night during the curtain call, two of the taller sixteen-year-old actors had to carry me out onstage on their shoulders so the audience could see me and give me the ovation they apparently thought I deserved. One evening early in the run, with the applause washing over me, one of the guys pinched my lederhosen-covered leg and said, "They love you, Robbie. You're pretty good at this." That this older guy, whom I idolized almost as much as I did Steve Allen, hinted I had a chance to do this for real further solidified my resolve to stick with acting for a little while.

LATER THAT YEAR, I had an *aha!* moment that convinced me that the world of theater was where I belonged.

Back in school, in my much hated algebra class, I looked up from the empty answer column of the test that I was probably flunking and glanced out the open door. The room was adjacent to the gym field, and, stumped by a particularly difficult equation, I craned my neck so I could see what was going on outside and was treated to a vision of the senior girls, clad in their sexy gym shorts, busy at their archery drills. Their targets were posted on bales of hay wet from a recent rain, and the scent of wet hay reminded me of the scene-paint odor that permeated the backstage area at the Teenage Drama Workshop. It made me pine for everything about the theater: the rehearsals, the performances, the applause, the making out with the girls who played the harem in *Aladdin.* I wasn't even fourteen, and I knew what I was going to do. There was no turning back. The decision was made for me. Everybody should be so lucky.

Throughout both junior high and high school, I took as many drama classes as possible. We were allowed to take drama electives as a replacement for English electives, which appealed to me because the stage was far more enjoyable than the classroom. I studied the history of playwriting, from the Greek comedies and tragedies, to Shakespeare, to contemporary theater. I did well enough that a couple of my teachers told me I qualified to be a teacher's assistant for credits, including a wonderful high school teacher, the character actor James Rawley, who played the mad scientist in the 1956 creepy cult classic *The Creature Walks Among Us*. (Considering my future in horror, it was ironic that I became the mad scientist's assistant. Hey, where's my hunchback?) But truthfully, the motives behind my desire to act weren't entirely pure. I had learned even in high school that it's far easier to meet girls when you're an actor.

Now, in those days, most boys didn't consider acting to be particularly cool—for that matter, the majority of the guys in my school thought we actors were sissies, believing if you didn't want to be a football player or an engineer, something was wrong with you—however, that meant the girl-to-guy ratio at your average drama party was about five to one, which was great news for yours truly.

I went to one of my first drama-class cast parties during my sophomore year. The hostess's parents were out of town, but even though we had the run of her house, we didn't have the typical get-as-drunk-as-you-possibly-can get-together because this wasn't the kind of girl who would throw a kegger; she was a "thespian." We're talking mixed drinks, and sophisticated older kids, including an openly gay bartender, with Cal Tjader albums spinning on the turntable. At this classy affair, nary an inebriated linebacker or puking shot-putter was to be seen. (A quick side note: I was also a surfer and a baseball player at the time, and the girl-to-guy ratio at the jock parties was about one to five.)

By the time I showed up, this very adult party was in full swing. The girls had blond hair, parted in the middle, ironed straight, Cleopatra eye makeup, and natural pre-pilates thin figures. They were wearing bikinis, floating in the shallow end of the pool, and sipping on drinks garnished with little umbrellas and slices of fresh fruit. I smiled and thought, *These drama kids sure know how to throw a party.*

I never told my surfing and baseball-playing pals the specifics about the bikinis and frou-frou drinks because I wanted to keep the whole thing to myself. Nonetheless, they were intrigued with what I was up to and sometimes showed up at my performances. Despite being thoroughly confused by our Nazi-centric version of *Julius Caesar*, some of my delinquent buddies realized that theater looked like fun and actually enrolled in a couple of drama classes on their own. So I guess I can take credit for saving a handful of young minds . . . which will hopefully make up for the legions of young fans I've terrorized over the years.

These parties were amusing diversions, but the acting came first. I was game to try anything. I've always desired to stretch on the stage or in front of the camera—horror, comedy, drama, whatever; as long as it's interesting, I'm interested. During my freshman year, I was asked to wear a pigeon costume and do some filler shtick during a junior girls' fashion show, which seemed like a plan because, as we all know, one of the ways to a young lady's heart is through her funny bone. Aside from the two zit-faced tech crew geeks up in the rafters—both of whom are now probably wealthy business associates of Bill Gates Jr.—

I was the only male in the production, so again, the odds of meeting a girl were in my favor. So there I was, hanging out backstage, sneaking looks at twenty-six wannabe models from the junior class bouncing around in their matching Maidenform bras and panties in between outfit changes . . . the whole time hidden inside that fucking pigeon get-up.

About a third of the way through the evening, it dawned on me that I could play the pigeon horny, which, considering what I was watching backstage, wasn't that much of a stretch. So I started chasing the girls around the stage, flapping my wings, humping their legs, and pretending to pigeon poop on a papier-mâché fountain. The sillier I got, the more the crowd cracked up; and the more the crowd laughed, the further I pushed it. A kind of rock-star power comes from making people laugh—or, as I found out a few decades later, making them scream with fright—that's indescribable. It's an ephemeral thing, and it's addictive, getting the perfect laugh or scream at the right moment. It was like a drug, even more seductive than a mai tai–clutching senior actress.

After the show, I sat in the dressing room—trying to be cool and not gawk at the girls in their underwear—thinking, *My God, how did I get here, how did this happen? This is like a dream.* Ahh, show business.

CHAPTER 2

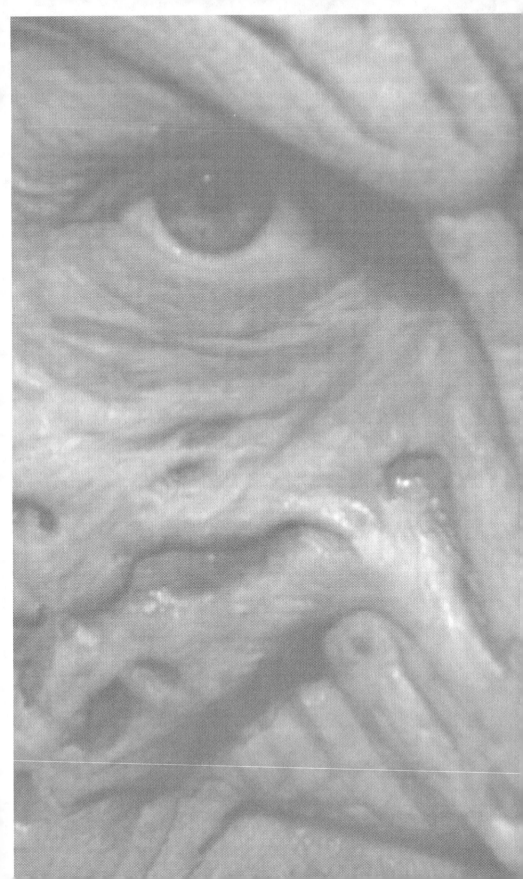

NIGHTMARE #2:

Stanley Kramer's film *The 5000 Fingers of Dr. T* was based on a story by Dr. Seuss. In the film, a high camera shot looks down on a giant grand piano, the object of a little boy's fear and dread of piano lessons. For years as a child, whenever I had a fever, I had a nightmare in which I was free-falling, spiraling down, down, down in slow motion toward that evil black piano. This dream haunted me until I was fifteen. Dr. Seuss had damaged me for life.

WHEN MY GRANDFATHER DIED, HE LEFT MY mother an apartment in Laguna Beach, and my family summered down there at some point most every year throughout my childhood. One summer, we invited my friend Stephanie from the Teenage Drama Workshop to join me, Mom, Dad, and my stepsister, Gail. The girls were dating a pair of brothers, both of whom were bona fide Newport Beach cool guys, both of whom I worshipped the same way in which I looked up to the older actors in the Workshop.

As was often the case when I was in my early teens, Gail had to drag me around whenever my parents went off to do their own thing. Fortunately, she and Stephanie liked having me around as a third wheel, especially when they were bored. They would amuse themselves by doing things like dyeing my hair platinum blond. I was actually okay with that, because even though I didn't surf at the time, I wanted to look like all the older surfer guys. I begged their boyfriends to teach me; since I was hanging around anyway, they reluctantly agreed to give me surfing lessons. I'd always been a good swimmer, so it was relatively easy for me to become a decent surfer. I kept working at it and kept improving, eventually evolving into a solid California surfer, somebody who'd earned his place in the lineup.

Surfing is one of those rare sports that's noncompetitive; it's you against yourself, you against the ocean. It's about balance and timing and knowing how to manipulate a floating object that glides across the face of a wave, a liquid wall that's collapsing across the surface of the sea. The ultimate free ride. Exhilarating. Kind of like acting.

My entry into surf culture couldn't have been timed better. During early high school, the most popular people were the football players and the cheerleaders, but by the time I was ready to go to college in 1965, the cool kids were the Beatles wannabes and us surfers. Times had changed, but I'd already done my changing, so socially speaking, I was in pretty good shape.

The surfing in California was good, but not always consistent. My crew liked to explore, so now and then we would sneak off down to Baja, Mexico to find better waves. None of our parents had any idea that we were outside of the country— I'm not sure what kind of excuses my friends came up with, but I'd generally tell my parents that we were camping up north of Malibu—and, God, if we'd been arrested south of the border, they would've had no clue where to look for us. With the omnipresent banditos, the bald tires on our '56 pickup, and the fact that often the person who drove was underage or inebriated, it's a wonder we didn't end up dead or in a Mexican jail.

My surfing buddies and I tended to get wrecked on beer, sake, shitty wine, and Mexican peach brandy. That's pretty much all we drank; we were so afraid of getting Montezuma's revenge that we refused to touch the water, choosing instead to throw down jug wine and all kinds of fruity alcohol. Of course, it being the midsixties, drugs were always around, but at first they didn't infiltrate our little group. The first time my surf crew smoked weed was during Easter break on one of our Mexican camping trips; we all huddled under a huge blanket so when we exhaled, we wouldn't lose any of the precious smoke. We were total weenies. Timothy Leary would've been embarrassed for us.

Then, right before high school graduation, much to everybody's surprise (mine included), I ran away from home. Walkedout. Just left. I got into an epic argument with my father.Part of it was inane—I believed that he'd reneged on his promise to pay my car insurance if I got good grades, and he believed it was my responsibility to pay my own damn car insurance—and part of it was deadly serious: he was pissed that I'd chosen to pursue acting rather than attend a good university and go to law school. Armed with the kind of righteous indignation that only an eighteen-year-old actor can muster, I threw my car keys at my father and stormed out of the house. It would be a while before I saw my parents again.

MY PLAN WAS TO go to college at California State University at Northridge. The college had an excellent drama school and a state-of-the-art stage tech department, plus, some of the old directors from the Teenage Drama Workshop were on the faculty. I was familiar with the campus, so I knew the transition would be fun and relatively easy. In the end, though, my decision to attend Cal State over the more prestigious

UCLA came down to two basic facts: one, I could afford it; and two, UCLA didn't allow freshmen on the stage, and I wasn't about to sit out a year.

That summer, I moved into the basement of an old Hollywood building where some of my drama department classmates and I were planning to start a summer theater. (The space, in Los Feliz, used to house an old beatnik poetry coffeehouse, and it must have been the most revered beatnik coffeehouse in the history of coffeehouses, as demonstrated by the map on the ceiling that featured the addresses and phone numbers of a network of beatnik coffeehouses across the country. What better place for a bunch of artistic types to convert into a temple of theater?) The other actors, many of whom had had similar battles with their own families, had no problem letting Rob Englund, the runaway, crash in the basement.

My best friend was an actor named Hugh Corcoran, and Hugh's family was minor Hollywood royalty. His sister Noreen was the costar of a hugely popular 1950s TV series called *Bachelor Father*, and his brother Kevin—who eventually became a producer on *The Shield*—had starred in *Old Yeller*, *Swiss Family Robinson*, and *Pollyanna* . . . not to mention that he was Moochie on the old *Mickey Mouse Club*. I was familiar with all their work and couldn't help but be quietly thrilled when they made me part of their family. Something was always simmering on the stove at the Corcorans', generally an enormous pot of Irish stew, and fascinating people were always coming and going in and out of the house, and they all treated me like an equal; I don't know if it was because Hugh told everybody that I had some talent, or if they were just being nice. But their motivations didn't matter to me—I was just happy to be there, chowing down, listening to stories about auditions, learning about the joys of cashing residual checks, overhearing gossip about Hollywood greats, and being invited to the sets of their respective television shows. That these accomplished people treated me as though I belonged gave me another layer of self-confidence that I took to the stage. As was the case after Steve Allen gave me that first taste of professional encouragement, I felt *included*.

Hugh and I became the managers of our little theater, which we dubbed Théâtre Intime, French for "intimate theater." That may sound pretentious, but it was more about marketing than anything else; that name was our way of putting a positive spin on our having only forty-six seats. We produced two summers of innovative theater and got rave reviews in the *L.A. Times*, *Variety*, and *Hollywood Reporter*—no small accomplishment because, at that time, there were just as many plays for journalists to review as there are today, with only a fraction of the media outlets. The highlights of our repertoire were our West Coast premieres of Arthur Miller's play about Marilyn Monroe, *After the Fall*, and Megan Terry's controversial antiwar piece, *Viet Rock*. Considering our tender ages, what we accomplished was incredible.

At the end of the summer, my father somehow tracked me down at the theater, and, rather than read me the riot act or threaten to disown me, he acted as if nothing had happened. He said he was glad to see me, gave me some money, and took me out for a steak, which was a welcome treat, as I'd survived the past year on coffee and French fries. I think he was impressed that I'd stuck to my guns. Once he realized how seriously I took my acting, he was proud, and that negated any residual anger or resentment . . . on both of our parts.

WHEN SCHOOL STARTED, I had little trouble assimilating. It didn't matter whether I was a surfer, a baseball player, a fighter pilot, or a drug dealer; when you go off to college, everybody starts at zero. You could be who you wanted to be. I wanted to be an actor. Fortunately, at that time, being an acting major at Cal State was just about the coolest thing you could be.

I knew right off the bat, just before my general audition for the drama department, that the acting scene in college was definitely going to be challenging. The young man who auditioned before me didn't look that intimidating—he was short and not anywhere near what you would call movie-star handsome—but the guy had talent. He strutted up onstage, stood confidently in front of the entire faculty, delivered a monologue from Edward Albee's *The Zoo Story*, and with seemingly no effort just fucking nailed it. This kid was passionate, he had presence, and he was original; I don't know if he could've handled the lead in *Pinocchio* or pulled off playing a randy pigeon, but this young man, this Richard Dreyfuss, was an Actor. With a capital *A*.

As I watched him knock one of my favorite monologues out of the park, I realized that if I was going to make any kind of mark in school—hell, if I was even going to *survive*—I had to step it up. The bar had been raised. As it happened, Richard wasn't long for Cal State, and he knew it. The day after my audition, he sidled over to me in the hall and whispered, "I've gotta get out of this place, and you should too." He dropped out soon thereafter and, within a few weeks, was doing improv comedy with Rob Reiner and, a few months after that, started popping up in TV shows such as *Bewitched*, *Gidget*, and *That Girl*. (Who knows—maybe I should've followed him to the Promised Land.)

One of my acting teachers during college was Jeff Corey. Jeff, who'd been blacklisted in the 1950s during Senator Joseph McCarthy's witch hunt, was the real deal and counted Jack Nicholson among his students. When I studied under him, Corey's career was on the upswing, and over the next few years he appeared in *Butch Cassidy and the Sundance Kid*, *True Grit*, and *Beneath the Planet of the Apes*. Between his film and television roles, he ran a challenging, unique master class in acting. I may have been a bit intellectually behind my other Corey classmates, but once I settled in and began to understand his language and philosophy, I was okay. He gave us a bunch of improv-oriented exercises that seemed to me to be well ahead of their time; for instance, he'd have two of us sit across the table from one another and hold off on our dialogue. We were supposed to just look at each other until some uncomfortable something—a funny blink of an eye or a suppressed burp—compelled one of us to begin the scene. On paper, that might not sound so exciting, but believe me, it gave us the skills to act more organically and observe and listen during a scene. But the truth is, much of what he taught me then didn't make practical sense until years later.

Another gentleman whose teachings confused me a bit while I was still in college was Lee Strasberg. One of the greatest gurus in acting history, Lee used to preach relaxation, relaxation, relaxation. He was all about "eliminating tension," and I didn't know what the fuck he was talking about until I was twenty-nine. The director had just called, "Action," during a particularly big scene in one of my first TV series when, without even thinking about it, I neglected to press my internal energy button and fell into a state of relaxation that was unlike anything I'd ever experienced either onstage or in front of the camera. I'd clicked into a mode that superseded my normal impulse to go a hundred miles an hour. I didn't have to work at manufacturing inner energy. I realized I could play a role excited even when I was feeling calm, and it gave me much more control over myself and the material. That was only a small tenet of Strasberg's method, and it's little surprise that the actors who studied with him for significant amounts of time—James Dean, Dustin Hoffman, Paul Newman, and Jane Fonda, among *many* others—turned out to be among the best of their respective generations.

Lee's classes were held in a movie theater in Westwood, and I studied alongside Shelley Winters and Lesley Ann Warren, as well as a number of other actors, writers, and directors who went on to have successful careers in Hollywood—and I was more than a little starstruck. I realized early on that a lot of what Lee was teaching only applied to working actors; novices such as me wouldn't get nearly as much out of the Strasberg Method as the pros. All the business about "sense memory" and "affective memory" and "protecting your character's agenda" didn't make sense to me at the time. But when it clicked in . . . well, suffice it to say that without Lee Strasberg—not to mention Jeff Corey and James Rawley—audiences wouldn't have believed in Freddy Krueger.

All of a sudden, school was in full swing, and things started getting serious. I'd initially gotten into acting for the girls and the adrenaline high—I didn't have an aesthetic agenda. But now, instead of splitting time between the surfers and the artists, I hung out almost exclusively with my fellow actors and ate, drank, and slept the theater. This wasn't considered mainstream behavior at that time. Good kids from good families weren't supposed to wear all black and yammer on about Pinter; we were fast-tracked to be doctors or engineers or businessmen, or—in the case of people with the gift of gab such as myself—lawyers. A nine-to-five job was respected. A hand-to-mouth job wasn't.

All this time with the drama crew was fine and good, but it wasn't doing a damn thing for my grade-point average, which was going down the toilet, primarily because we didn't get credit units for any of our stage appearances. I was barely attending any nondrama classes anyway, and zero plus zero equals zero. It looked as if I wasn't destined to get a diploma. So not only was I not going to be a lawyer, I wasn't even going to earn a college degree. My parents were less than impressed.

Near the end of that semester, I reconnected with my old high school sweetheart, Betsy, who was working at Cal State. The timing was right and we fell in love again. I was mature enough to appreciate true love, so I asked her to marry me. She said yes. I was twenty-one, close to being kicked out of school, and I was about to take my bride.

* * *

THAT SPRING, ONE OF my friends went to England to audition for the Royal Academy of Dramatic Art, one of the most prestigious training grounds for actors in the entire world. When he came back, he told me the RADA faculty was holding auditions at Mills College, a small school up in Oakland. Now between the Teenage Drama Workshop, high school, Théâtre Intime, and Cal State, I'd performed in almost fifty plays and I had a number of solid audition pieces ready to go, so I figured I'd give it a try. Four of my actor friends also wanted to give RADA a shot, so, fueled on coffee and uppers, we piled into our hippie-mobile and hauled ass up to the Bay Area.

About halfway there, we stopped at a kitschy, Catskills-like honeymoon motel called the Madonna Inn to use the toilet and grab some food, because we realized it was foolish to rely entirely on stimulants to get us up to Oakland and through our auditions. The highlight of my Madonna Inn experience was the bathroom, where, after pissing about six gallons of coffee, I experienced my first automatic electronic-eye flush toilet. After I played with the urinal for a while, I zipped up, and it dawned on me that the bathroom had some of the best acoustics I'd ever heard, so I told my friends they needed to get in there and start running their lines because they'd never sound better. After about thirty minutes of practicing in the john, we piled back into the car and kept heading north.

We finally made it to Mills College and immediately realized that this was just about the worst place we could possibly audition because the distractions were myriad. Turned out that Mills was an all-girls school. While I was trying to brush up on my Shakespeare, every hot coed in northern California was either sunbathing on the campus lawn or walking around in black tights and no bra. Between the speed, and the girls, and the long drive, I was a mess.

The old theater where the auditions were held had great acoustics, almost as good as the crapper at the Madonna Inn. My friends and I paced up and down the creaky aisles, warmed up our voices, practiced our lines, and did our best to calm our nerves.

Then it was time to do my thing.

What felt like the entire RADA faculty sat in the front row, wearing their turtlenecks and tweedy jackets, looking oh-so-English. Feeling equally European in my head-to-toe corduroy outfit and work boots, I presented myself as professionally as possible, offered up my name, introduced my audition pieces, and went to work. The rest is a blank. I know I rushed my lines a bit—no surprise, considering all the caffeine coursing through my bloodstream—and I recall getting a single laugh, but that's it. After I finished, one of the faculty members told me that he liked my energy. (Thank you, pills and coffee.) I waited while my friends read their monologues, then we all headed back south.

The letters showed up a few weeks later. That year, out of nearly nine hundred who auditioned, only fifteen were invited to train at RADA. Three of that fifteen were from my little group. So just like that, it was off to London. Or so we thought.

Several months prior, RADA had apparently become embroiled in a huge controversy about teaching methodology. Long story short, the old schoolers didn't like the touchy-feely avant-garde direction the new schoolers were headed in, and the new schoolers wanted the old schoolers to get hip. The traditionalists got fed up with the whole thing, left RADA, and headed to the United States, in search of a university in a community with an arts budget that could support a professional acting-training school. What better location than the American Midwest—Rochester, Michigan, home of Oakland University?

So much for swinging London.

CHAPTER
3

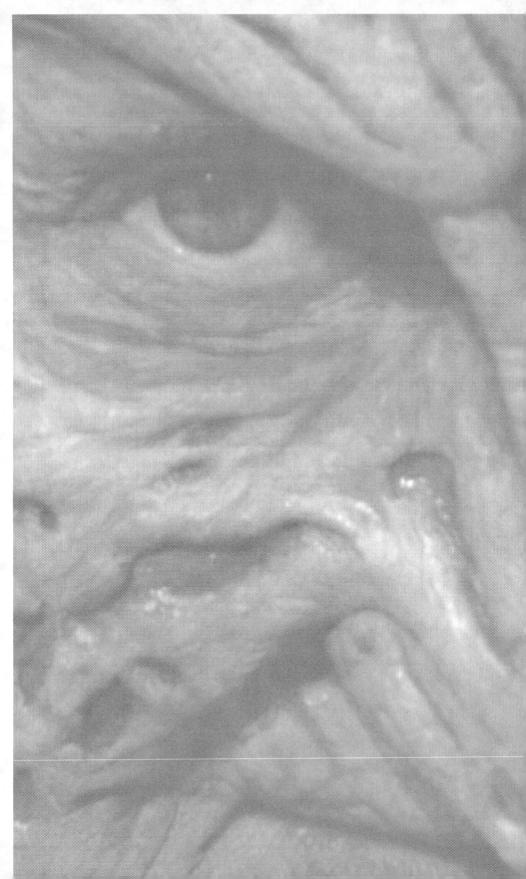

NIGHTMARE #3:

I find myself in the hills of Griffith Park, the massive urban park that divides East Hollywood, Los Angeles, and the Valley. I'm not sure of my age; I could be at a Cub Scout outing or attending a hippie love-in during my early college years. I'm on a rough cut hiking path on a steep slope. There are scattered oak trees and chaparral flanking me. I'm running. I'm in control and dodging large rocks, roots, and holes. Suddenly I'm accelerating, going faster. I lose control; it's as if my legs and gravity have taken over. My heart rate quickens, I can't catch my breath. As I barrel downhill on the uneven trail I see a coiled rattlesnake thirty yards ahead of me. I can't stop. I'm going too fast. I use my momentum to vault over the rattler. I never look back. My pounding heart awakens me.

AKLAND UNIVERSITY WAS CALLED "THE Harvard of the Midwest," which was a slight exaggeration. But while OU might not have been in the Ivy League, it had one hell of an arts program, a whole lot of wealthy alumni, and a gorgeous professional theater called the Meadow Brook. So those canny Englishmen drew up some paperwork, pulled some strings, and opened up the Academy of Dramatic Art, a two-year acting school helmed by the newly arrived faculty from the Royal Academy of Dramatic Art. RADA became ADA.

The teachers all lived on the Matilda Dodge Wilson Estate at the forested edge of the Oakland campus. That's *Dodge* as in "Dodge cars," and that's *Dodge cars* as in "We have enough money to build a Tudor-style mansion with the largest indoor horse-riding arena in the world." The university welcomed the RADA gang with open arms and an open pocketbook; they so wanted the Brits to feel at home that they allowed them to convert a stable into a twenty-four-hour pub, complete with a Union Jack flying in front of it.

So at the end of the summer of 1968, Betsy and I packed our things and drove out to Michigan. I was going to be an actor, she was going to be a medical secretary, and it was all a huge adventure into the great unknown. Even though the United States seemed to be falling apart around us—we're talking the Martin Luther King and Bobby Kennedy assassinations and the riots at the Democratic National Convention in Chicago—we couldn't have been happier. When we hit Rochester, I immediately went to work, and after nearly flunking out of a school where I had lost interest in academic theater, ADA was nirvana. The training, the discipline, rehearsing and performing a different classical play every six weeks—it was everything I'd hoped it would be.

One of the first things I realized when I got to Oakland University was that in terms of social life, I'd landed my butt in a tub of butter. At RADA in the UK, I'm sure it would've been go to class, go to rehearsal, go home, do it again. But at ADA in Michigan, we went to class, went to rehearsal, then went to the pub and drank and bullshitted with the teachers—and we're talking teachers who'd mentored the likes of Peter O'Toole, Albert Finney, and Alan Bates—into the wee hours. Then back to classes again the next morning, and in the evening we'd go to the Meadow Brook Theatre and work in any capacity, from techie, to spear carrier, to understudy. My first paying job at the Meadow Brook was a combination of understudying a small role in a George Bernard Shaw play, and backstage janitor; even if I was lucky enough to get on the stage, I'd still have to mop it up at the end of the night. But I was becoming a professional in the world that I loved.

ADA was a novel training program and attracted the attention of the country's most prestigious drama educators. John Houseman, for example, sat in on several classes to pick up concepts and curriculum he could take back to his students at the new Juilliard acting school—the same Juilliard that Kevin Kline, Christopher Reeve, Robin Williams, and Patty LuPone would attend the following year.

Inspired by the artistic aura of the place, I thrived on the discipline. Every morning, I would train by myself before class: voice work, ballet exercises, memorization. Meanwhile, the teachers—these fifty- and sixtysomethings who'd been theater professionals for their entire adult lives—began embracing the culture of sixties America, most notably marijuana and the new independent cinema. There we were, eager students, trying to sound like Laurence Olivier, and there they were, all falling in love with Marlon Brando, Steve McQueen, and Thai stick. It was the ultimate in weird role reversal, but it certainly made our trips to the pub that much more interesting. Once they'd tipped a few gin and tonics, our tutors became quite expansive with their storytelling, regaling us with tales about hanging out on Broadway with a *very* young Julie Andrews, and performing Shakespeare with Richard Burton, and Albert Finney's notorious talents as a cocksman. It was an utterly romantic and magical time.

LATE SPRING BETWEEN MY first and second years at ADA, I made my first pilgrimage to New York City to audition for summer stock theater; nobody was at the Academy during July and August, and I wasn't about to sit around Middle-of-Nowhere, Michigan, twiddling my thumbs. I showed up at my first New York audition looking like a Dickensian street urchin, clad in a John Lennon cap, a scarf, tight jeans, Beatle boots, and a peacoat. Despite my outfit, many of the casting people seemed to like me, specifically the fine folks from the Penn State Summer Theater, who offered me small parts in a couple of plays. Four hours later, I went to a second audition, this one for the Great Lakes Shakespeare Festival in Cleveland, and they offered me even bigger roles. Two auditions, two offers. It wasn't Broadway, but it'd do.

Afterward, I met up with an old friend from junior high school, Gary Tigerman, who had become a working actor and lived in Greenwich Village. (Gary had scripted my infamous pigeon performance at the high school fashion show, and starred as Mark Antony in our Nazi-centric production of *Julius Caesar*.) This was my first time in the Village, and it blew me away. Every other shop sold psychedelic gear, and there was some infamous jazz club every few blocks, such as the Village Gate or Slugs. I thought that Gary, who was starring on Broadway, was the luckiest guy in the world.

We went back to his place, which was a dumbbell apartment—i.e., two big-ish rooms connected by a long, skinny hall. He gave me the grand tour (such as it was), which concluded in his bedroom, where, on a giant water bed that covered two-thirds of the room, lay his girlfriend, an actress named Janice Fisher. Jan, who was recovering from surgery, looked vaguely familiar to me. She, however, *immediately* recognized me as the actor who'd played Pinocchio in the Teenage Drama Workshop, the kid whom she'd had a crush on that summer long ago. It's a small world after all.

Jan climbed out of her sickbed—or sick water bed, more accurately—because she decided that it was her mission to show me Manhattan. For the next several weeks, it was Fellini movie premieres, and watching Katharine Hepburn on Broadway from the wings, and postperformance drinks with the cast of *Jesus Christ Superstar*. Meanwhile, my friends from Michigan and I were taking in Broadway plays, most memorably the original production of Stephen Sondheim's *Company*, a musical that I considered so far ahead of its time that it put so-called radical works such as *Hair* to shame. I thought of myself as a "classical" actor now, an Anglophile, and somewhat of a theater snob, but this modern American musical rocked my world. I realized art could be contemporary, meaningful, and popular, all at the same time.

As the week progressed, it became evident that Jan and I had a connection. We didn't kiss. We didn't sleep together. All we did was walk the streets of Manhattan and talk, talk, talk. We formed a bond, but nothing could happen romantically because I was married, and she was living with one of my oldest friends. Sounds like the plot of a corny Broadway musical.

And this was all in ten days.

I ARRIVED BACK IN Michigan full of big-city culture, with a summer job at the Great Lakes Shakespeare Festival in my back pocket, and right away things got rolling. I earned my Equity card and appeared in play after play after play, and I started making some real, honest-to-goodness money. Meanwhile, my wife, Betsy, was getting politicized; she'd helped organize a nurses' union at the hospital where she worked. Our worlds were radically different: she was involved and altruistic, and I was insulated in the fantasy world of the theater. We were still very much in love, but it's possible that she looked at me as somebody who was more self-indulgent than he should've been. It might not have been the best time to leave her in Detroit and go down to Cleveland to work on my Shakespearean chops, but I had to follow the work.

Rather than room with other actors in Ohio, I rented my own apartment in the hopes that Betsy would come and join me for a few weeks later in the season. Since I was on my own, I immersed myself in the work and drew from my ADA training and discipline. When Betsy did finally come down for a visit and saw how hard I was working, and how serious I was about my profession, it finally dawned on her that this might be our life together: me in a different city every couple of months, focusing the majority of my energy on my craft. I think she wondered then if that kind of life would make her happy.

After an exhilarating season in Cleveland, it was back to Michigan, where I continued my studies and was invited to join the repertory company at the Meadow Brook Theatre. I also became a member of the faculty and taught an adjunct class in stage combat and period technique, where I demonstrated how to properly faint (it goes knees, hips, elbows), throw a convincing punch (it's all in the eyes), and how to remain butch while wearing a wig and mincing about in tights and high heels (don't ask). I was busy, but I was also hungry, and I wanted more.

Toward the end of the season—a season in which I thought I'd gone above and beyond the call of duty, professionally speaking, at one point playing six different roles in a single play—I was promised a crack at the lead role in our final show, *The Glass Menagerie*. I coveted that role, probably more than any other role in my short career. The part ended up going to the director's boy toy, some actor from Lincoln Center, and I felt entirely betrayed. I had no idea (or maybe I'd chosen not to believe) that politics were involved in this sort of thing. I always thought of the theater as a pure place. Wrong. Lesson learned. I graduated ADA with honors, and it was time to move on.

THE FOLLOWING SUMMER, I went back to Cleveland to do some more Shakespeare, but I stumbled into a couple of other projects, most notably the musical *Godspell.* It was a huge hit, standing room only. I played Judas, and people noticed. Especially the girls.

Soon after the show opened, there was a party in Cleveland to celebrate the release of the *Godspell* soundtrack, and even though we weren't on the album, the principals in our cast were invited. In true record industry fashion, some . . . shall we say, ladies of the evening were invited, all of whom were available to Jesus and his disciples at no charge. These working girls looked like the Supremes. I'd never been with a Motown diva and I succumbed. I mean, how many times do you get the opportunity to do a Supreme?

For the first time, I had groupies. I met more than one novice nun from a local convent who wanted to sacrifice her virginity to Judas. Turns out even nuns want the bad boy. Once I mentioned during a radio interview that I liked Michelob, and the next night a couple young ladies left three cases of beer on my doorstep. There were flowers and love letters and poems and drawings. It was stardom on a small scale—pretty heady stuff, which I embraced, most notably the hedonistic side . . . all while my wife was up in Michigan.

Betsy and I had fallen in love in high school and married young, but now we were in our midtwenties, and we weren't anything like the people we were when we first met, so when she met me in Cleveland, things felt a bit off-kilter. But the love was still there, so when I was invited to join *Godspell* off-Broadway, I turned it down, opting instead to return to Michigan for another season at Meadow Brook. I was still smarting from *The Glass Menagerie* disappointment and wasn't happy with the season in general, but I sucked it up, did three plays, taught a few classes, and tried my best to salvage my marriage.

One night I was doing some channel surfing, and I happened across a movie called *Boxcar Bertha*. *Boxcar* was Martin Scorsese's directorial debut, starred Barbara Hershey and David Carradine, and was produced by Hollywood's most savvy schlockmeister, Roger Corman. It was a good enough film, but what I noticed were the closing credits: it seemed as though half the crew and a few bit players had been my compadres back at Cal State and at Théâtre Intime.

Hmm.

So there I am, sitting in Bumfuck, Michigan, snow up to my ass, frustrated with the whole Meadow Brook scene, spending more time teaching than acting, navigating the rocks with Betsy, and it hit me—if I was going to deal with the bullshit politics of acting, I might as well do it in Hollywood, where at least the pay is better. My romance with the world of classical theater had faded. It was hard for me to acknowledge my naïve notion that the theater was a sacred temple of art. And my thinking was that if my college friends had made peace with commercial Hollyweird, I could too. It was time to go home.

I drove west with two of my Academy buddies, which was an adventure in and of itself. When we got to Reno, one of my traveling partners—who considered himself somewhat of a cardshark—took a chunk of our gas money and hit the blackjack tables. For a starving actor like me, a guy who was saving all his money to rent an apartment for him and his wife, this was blasphemy. But the guy won big. We treated ourselves to Bloody Marys and gorged on filet mignon, eggs, orange juice, and hash browns. This first real meal we'd had in a week gave us the energy to make it to Los Angeles without stopping.

We rolled into my parents' driveway at midnight, completely exhausted. I banged on the door, surprised the hell out of Mom and Dad, and just like that a new chapter of my life began.

CHAPTER
4

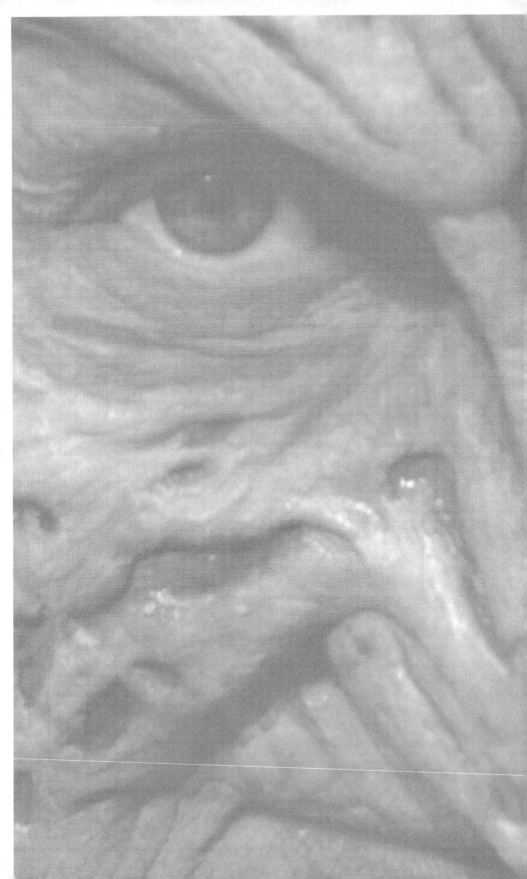

NIGHTMARE #4:

While summering at the seashore with my parents, I
wandered into a late-afternoon double-bill matinee at the
local movie house. The first half was a kiddie flick, but the
second feature was a World War II movie, *The Naked and
the Dead*, based on the famous novel by Norman Mailer.
This gritty, adult war drama captivated me until a sequence
when a young GI grunt is bitten by a poisonous, lime green
snake and dies horribly. The soldier writhed in pain, and
the snake's poison bubbled and foamed from his mouth,
nose, and eyes. After he died, one of his buddies found the
giant green reptile and hacked it to pieces. For the rest of
the summer, I checked under the bed in our rented beach
house for snakes. And for the next ten years, I played host
to the violent images from that film enhanced by my own
imagination in the nightmares I suffered as a result of that
summer day in a dark, dark, dark movie theater.

AFTER CRASHING WITH MY PARENTS FOR A couple of days, I put a deposit on a one-room bungalow managed by one Cliff Coleman. When I found out that Cliff was one of Sam Peckinpah's longtime assistant directors, I knew I was officially home— after all, in Hollywood, *everybody*'s in the industry.

The tiny cottage was right on the sand by the Santa Monica Pier, a charming little joint I thought would be a perfect place for Betsy and me to recharge our marriage. We spent much of the summer enjoying the beach, surfing, catching up with old friends, collecting unemployment, and resting and recuperating. Along with some actor friends who followed me out from Michigan, I took weekly three-hour acting classes with an actor/director/concentration-camp survivor named Jack Garfein, figuring at the very least I'd meet some professional, working actors who could help me get a gig or two. I also needed to get back into the Hollywood loop; after being immersed in the classics, I felt I could do with an infusion of contemporary showbiz.

Before long, Betsy and I realized that things weren't working out. We'd married too young, and we'd grown too far apart to repair and rebuild our relationship, so we agreed to separate; then, a few months later, we got a do-it-yourself divorce. We ended on good terms. No lasting damage. We just changed. That's sometimes the way it goes.

I soon learned that my New York friends Jan and Gary had also moved back home, to a place in the Hollywood foothills across the street from Frank Lloyd Wright's son's Batcave-looking house. They were huge film fanatics, and we all spent a lot of time at cheap movie matinees or in front of the television, checking out old and new films of all genres. With every movie, my respect for the medium grew.

Gary had registered as a conscientious objector and was forced to serve, in effect, community service for the government. The government sent him up to the NASA test center in the Bay Area, where, as an experiment, he had to remain in bed for six months. I'm not sure how watching an actor lie around for half a year helped the good old USA, but what do I know? Thank God it wasn't me. It could've been a nightmare on Skylab.

WITHOUT GARY, IT BECAME difficult for Jan and their other roommate to foot the rent, so they asked me to move in. Their friends all seemed to be in the industry: actors, cameramen, choreographers, and future film critics, and it further immersed me in the culture of Hollywood. This entire crowd ate, drank, and slept movies, but couldn't afford to see new films, so we did what many enterprising, young starving artists did in the early 1970s: we crashed studio screenings. And we were so slick that we never got caught.

Over the next year, I rediscovered and again fell in love with American cinema and spent many an evening at the local revival theater, watching a Billy Wilder double feature, or a couple of Hitchcock films, or back-to-back film noirs. A revival schedule was always tacked up on the wall by the telephone, with all the titles we wanted to see over the next several weeks highlighted in red.

Considering our dovetailing tastes, our proximity to one another, and that Gary and Jan had been having problems before he was sent to San Francisco, it was all but inevitable that Jan and I would fall into a relationship. Even though it was wrong on a certain level, we couldn't *not* fall into each other's arms. Sometimes these things are meant to happen. You can't help it, and you can't fight it. Gary and Jan eventually officially broke up, and Jan and I officially became an item.

I went on my first real Hollywood audition in early 1973 for a film called *Buster and Billie,* starring Jan-Michael Vincent, who was one of Hollywood's true rising stars at the time, having come off of the hit Charles Bronson movie *The Mechanic,* as well as the Disney classic *The World's Greatest Athlete.* He was being groomed as the next James Dean/Steve McQueen, and if I managed to land a job in this movie—a movie that was going to be in the tradition of Peter Bogdanovich's recent successful period piece, *The Last Picture Show*—it would be huge.

I read for the role of Whitey, the classic sidekick, an albino southerner, and the third male lead. And I got it, beating out Gary Busey. (Gary was young and calm then; if I'd taken a part from him at any point after, say, 1983, who knows what would've happened?) My salary: about $5,000. Not exactly Freddy Krueger money, but at the time that paycheck was damn welcome.

Not only was Whitey an albino, but he was a self-conscious

albino who so despised his affliction that he dyed his hair with black shoe polish. A few weeks before the shoot kicked off, I went to see the makeup man, and more than anything else, he was concerned about my hair. He took me to see the studio wig expert, a little Russian lady who had a cluster of Emmy Awards on her mantel. At the back of her ranch house—which, from the inside, looked like a Russian Orthodox church—was a room with dozens of wigheads topped with toupees. Since she was the best in town, rugs of every variety were on display, some of which had been worn by the likes of John Wayne and Rip Torn. She took one look at my blond surfer ringlets and decided that dye wouldn't work, so she ducked into an annex and came back with a jet-black crew-cut toupee, plopped it on my head, and said, "Perfect!"

She was right. It looked great. But it had an odd smell about it. "Has somebody worn this recently?"

"No," she said. "The last time it was used was four years ago. Alan Arkin wore it in *Catch-22*."

Now *that* was cool. Smelly, but cool.

BUSTER AND BILLIE WAS shot in Allman Brothers country, outside a tiny Georgia town called Statesboro. On our first day there we went to a pancake breakfast held by the local Rotarians, who ran the town. It was a can't-miss event—especially for the big star Jan-Michael—because we needed to butter up the townsfolk to get cheaper rates for our film locations. This was my first lesson on how to stretch your film dollar, which prepared me for the myriad budget restrictions on the early *Nightmare* movies, as well as the tight budgets on movies I would later direct.

A few days before we'd left for Georgia, I'd been shuttled over to the studio-appointed optometrist in Beverly Hills, who was going to measure me for a pair of albino-like pink contact lenses. The lenses arrived in town right after the Rotary Club breakfast, and I had to try them on immediately because shooting started that afternoon. The contacts were kind of big, so big that it felt as if teacup saucers were under my eyelids, and I immediately started tearing up. Another problem: the lenses were red, which would theoretically make my eyes look pink. Unfortunately, my eyes are light green, and when you mix red and green, you get brown. When I got to the set, despite being scared shitless I'd get thrown off the movie if I complained about *anything*, I told our director, Daniel Petrie— an A-lister who'd directed *A Raisin in the Sun*—that the lenses were causing problems. "I can't act in these. I just can't. Maybe you can't see it, but I feel like I'm crying all the time. What can we do, Dan?"

Without hesitation he said, "Take 'em out. The eyes are the windows of the soul, and I want the audience to see *your* eyes, not some contact lenses. Nobody's going to care if you don't have pink eyes." So I immediately took 'em out, and, man, was I grateful. I'd learned a valuable lesson: stick to your guns. Dan smiled, went back behind the camera, shouted, "Action," and away we went.

Our female lead, Pamela Sue Martin, was one of the most gorgeous creatures in creation: porcelain skin, a willowy body, and large, expressive eyes. That she was talented made her that much more desirable. During the shoot, she caught a brutal cold, but even with a runny nose and red, swollen eyes she was still one of the most beautiful women I'd ever seen. (Even if I had developed a crush on Pamela—which I didn't—I wouldn't have made a move because (a) I had a girlfriend, and (b) said girlfriend had come on location with me.)

Statesboro was a dry town, and the only place we could get a drink was at the local American Legion. And it wasn't as if we could get beer or wine; all they had to offer us was homemade moonshine. And that was some quality moonshine—come 2002, that same stuff would bring $10 a shot in a high-end New York City cocktail lounge.

If we had a taste for something other than 'shine, we had to find a way to get to the next county. One night, Jan-Michael had a craving for Cuervo Gold, so he stole one of the film's 1940s-era prop cars and hauled ass across the county line to the nearest package-liquor store, justifying his behavior by saying, "This is what my character would do." That sounded good to me, so I went along for the wild ride, which took us right across the local college football field. Somehow we managed not to get arrested. Talk about Method acting. Lee Strasberg would've been thrilled.

MY PERFORMANCE IN *BUSTER AND BILLIE* got great reviews—*Time* magazine said, "*Buster and Billie* contains some good acting, especially by a boy named Robert Englund, who plays Buster's best friend"—and its success helped me get a number of prestigious auditions, most notably one for the role of Telly Savalas's sidekick in the series *Kojak*. (Apparently I had a sidekick look about me.) After about a half-dozen callbacks, I was told I didn't get it, which got me to thinking about the entire Hollywood audition process.

I realized that sometimes you've won or lost the part before you utter a single word of dialogue. Your blond hair might land you the role, while your height (or lack thereof) might help that tall guy you rode up in the elevator with get the part. I also realized that getting called back is a triumph itself, and even if I didn't get a certain part, I should still feel good that somebody in the casting office, or several somebodies, liked me well enough to give me a second, or third, or even a tenth shot. You have to turn the negative into a positive and take what you can out of the experience, and that could be something as small as a good acting tip, or something as big as getting the producer's contact number. At the very least, staying positive helps you stay sane.

It also dawned on me that there are two kinds of film roles: those you do for the money and the work, and those you do for artistic fulfillment. But every once in a while, something comes along that could be both lucrative and fulfilling, such as the film I auditioned for in 1973 called *The Last Detail*, which starred Jack Nicholson. I was in the running for the part of the young sailor that Jack and his navy buddy were escorting to the brig, a meaty, possibly career-making role. The role went to Randy Quaid—an actor I admire and who did a brilliant job in the film—but losing it still haunts me. (A few years later, a gentleman wandered over to me in a movie-theater lobby and told me how much he liked my work in *Buster and Billie* and

Stay Hungry. This was Darryl Ponicsan, the guy who wrote both the novel and the screenplay for *The Last Detail.* All I could think was *Why weren't you at one of my auditions?!*)

What somewhat softened the blow was that the following year I landed a small but crucial part in *Hustle,* a contemporary film noir with an all-star cast featuring Catherine Deneuve, Ernest Borgnine, and the man who at that time was arguably Hollywood's biggest star, Burt Reynolds. This was a top-notch project—pancake breakfasts with the locals wouldn't be required—but the coolest aspect was that I was to play the guy who kills Burt Reynolds.

The day of Burt's impending death, we were on location at a liquor store in Pasadena. The prop man handed me the gun, and I was suddenly nervous because, even though I had my stage combat down cold, I'd never before fired a gun in a movie. Making matters more difficult, the camera angle was strange, an extreme close-up of the gun barrel pointing at Burt's head, and I knew that if the shot was going to work, I'd need to point the gun just slightly away from his face. No problem. Unfortunately, the prop man made a mistake that almost cost Burt his face, and me my career.

When I went to plug Burt, I had no idea that the gun was packed with twice as much load as necessary, so when the director shouted, "Action," and I pulled the trigger, Burt's toupee flapped in the breeze from the discharge—thank God it didn't blow off completely. The disintegrated paper from the blank charge went all over him and his wardrobe; it looked like he'd had a massive attack of dandruff. I felt like the biggest weenie on the set. I wondered if I'd ever work in this town again.

Burt wiped all the crap off his face, put his arm around my

shoulders, and pulled me off to the side. "Look, kid," he said, "don't feel bad."

"I don't feel bad. I feel *terrible*."

"These things happen. No big deal. I'm okay. Listen, when we do it again, I want you to get vicious and look psychotic. This is my big death scene. The nastier you are, the more the audience will care about me." The second take, everything went off without a hitch, and Mr. Reynolds was dead. I've killed plenty of people in my film career, but Burt was my first movie star.

(A side note: even though the scene ended up fine, I was still a bit down after work, so on the way home I stopped at a bar for a quick one . . . or two . . . I couldn't decide what to order, but I remembered that throughout *Hustle*, Burt's character drinks an Irish whiskey called Old Bushmills. I'd never tasted it, but it was love at first sip. For the next twenty-five years, it was my poison of choice.)

THE FOLLOWING YEAR, I went up to Bellingham, Washington, a blue-collar town north of Seattle, to film *Young Joe, the Forgotten Kennedy*, a TV movie about Joseph Kennedy Jr. I had a featured role, which afforded me plenty of downtime, most of which was passed hiding from the constant rain inside the one decent bar in town. The bar was always filled with young women flying solo because all of their husbands were up in the far north working on the Alaskan Pipeline. They were lonely, flush with their absent hubby's money, and we were bored, horny actors with time to kill, so naturally the party was on.

On our first Friday night in Washington, the party moved from the bar to one of our cast member's suites and soon got wild. To set the mood, I grabbed some shirts off the floor and tossed them over the lampshades, which I hoped would create some mellow party lighting, then jacked up the stereo and made sure that everybody in the room had some tequila. Always the gracious host.

So everybody's drinking and making out and having a good old time, and there, in the center of the scrum, one of our actors was dancing with one of the local gals. They were grinding closer and closer, and it was getting hotter and hotter, and all of a sudden, right there, in the middle of the party, the guy gave her a *very* healthy backhand and everything went silent, except for the horrible disco tune pumping from the speakers.

A couple of the other cast members ran over to restrain their actor friend before things could get further out of hand. At that moment the gal stepped up to the actor and nailed him with a roundhouse punch. The actor slowly smiled. Then the gal, with her bloody split lip, grinned right back at him. He planted a kiss on her, a passionate, sexy, bloody kiss. They disappeared into the fluorescent-lit bathroom and closed the door behind them. They weren't seen for the rest of the weekend, and they remained a couple until the shoot was over. A match made in hell. I was growing up fast.

A couple of months later, I auditioned for a costarring role in another big movie with an all-star cast—Jeff Bridges, Sally Field, Arnold Schwarzenegger, and Scatman Crothers, among others—called *Stay Hungry*. For the first time in my career,

I went to the interview in character, which basically meant resurrecting the southern accent I'd used in *Buster and Billie*. Several callbacks later, I was offered the part, beating out Sylvester Stallone and, for the second time in four years, Gary Busey. (Probably because of our early typecasting as southerners, Gary and I went up for the same roles a lot back in the seventies. Some of them he got, some of them I got, and I have no hard feelings whatsoever because I love his work. I have no idea how he feels about mine, and frankly, I don't want to find out.)

Originally, I was only scheduled to shoot in Alabama for six weeks on *Stay Hungry*. But the director, Bob Rafelson, was working his magic, and magic is sometimes slow in coming, so I wound up on location for almost three months, with pockets full of per diem and many unscheduled hours to fill in the Deep South.

Scatman was my next-door neighbor at the motel, and one dull night I was awakened by a whole lot of banging on his door. I peeked my head into the hallway and saw three huge policemen, pounding away. As a Californian and the child of liberal parents, I imagined the worst: in 1977, southern cops plus a black man wouldn't likely add up to anything good.

After shooting several films below the Mason-Dixon line, I've come to love the South and southerners—the hospitality, the sultry nights, the food, and the music are all unique, and I have also realized that down there, whites and blacks probably have more positive daily interaction than they do up north. Still, back at that motel in Alabama, I figured that nothing good would come of the police action next door. I just hoped that Scatman didn't have any weed.

A few minutes later the cops pulled out their billy clubs, kicked the door in, and rushed into the room. As I listened to the ruckus next door, I remembered that Scatman had wrapped the day before and was probably at home back in Los Angeles. I peeked out my window and saw Alabama's finest dragging two rednecks out the door. Ironically, it turned out the only people the local police force was prejudiced against were criminals. Chalk one up for white guilt.

Working with Sally Field was a joy. Not only was she a fine actress, but she was cute; and who would've guessed that the Flying Nun had such a hot, sexy little body. Sally and I used to ride from the hotel to the set in these enormous station wagons, the kind of car that every other suburban family owned, circa 1975. Sally loved pop music—strictly AM radio; FM wasn't quite on her radar—and she knew the lyrics to every tune on the Top 40. So every morning, without fail, we'd get into the car, Sally would ask me to hold her coffee while she tuned the radio to her favorite local station, and then she'd sing along with damn near everything. When some actors want to get into the zone, they meditate or do breathing exercises. When Sally wanted to get into the zone, she belted out "Sugar, Sugar."

Not only did I have a good ol' time during filming, but I learned a lot on the set. One of the things I'm proudest of is my one-take five-bank pool shot filmed in the master. Today, that would be the kind of thing that would most likely be CGI'ed in postproduction, but back then, I had to learn how to make that shot, and learn it quickly, because I didn't want to be the guy who added another costly day to the shooting schedule.

For some fans, the highlight may have been the fight in the gym scene when I took a pool cue in the balls. I think that was the second greatest nut-shot in cinema history, number one being when Paul Newman booted one of his gang in the groin in *Butch Cassidy and the Sundance Kid.* That one you could feel all the way in the balcony.

Schwarzenegger had brought in seemingly every body-builder in the world to appear in the film's last scenes, featuring a weight-lifting contest. These guys were ripped, and my lasting image of that location was dozens of these magnificent physical specimens diving into our motel's pool from the third-story roof. Now *that* was a wrap party!

SOON AFTER *STAY HUNGRY* wrapped, thanks to the money I'd saved up from my film work, Jan and I finally moved into our own place in the foothills above Studio City, a beautiful apartment building that had been designed by master architect Rudolph Schindler. We continued to socialize with our coterie of film geeks, one of whom introduced us to a funny young actor whom we liked so much we practically adopted him. His name was Mark Hamill.

Mark, who was an eye blink away from becoming Luke Skywalker, became a fixture in our Schindler apartment, and even though he was only a few years younger than Jan and me, he was a lot more attuned to contemporary pop culture. He introduced me to Monty Python, as well as a bunch of little-known sci-fi and horror movies. (Mark was a serious horror fanatic, complete with a subscription to *Famous Monsters* magazine.) He was a die-hard fan of *The Mary Tyler Moore Show*, and he loved his Heineken. Mark clued me in to quality TV, and introduced me to the delights of watching old Marx Brothers movies in the middle of the afternoon. Simply put, he helped me to lighten up.

My agent sent me up to read for the part of the surfer in *Apocalypse Now*. I wore an old khaki, thrift-store army shirt, faded green Levi's, and work boots to the audition in an effort to look military, because going to auditions in character was working for me. They took one look at me and decided I was too old. (Truth be told, I was more interested in the part of the cook that Frederic Forrest eventually played, but I was too young for that one.) "But," one of the casting people suggested, "you might want to poke your head into the door across the hall. They're working on something you might be right for."

And that something was *Star Wars*.

But again my age was a factor; I was too young to play Han Solo. I left the building, went to the Formosa, my favorite watering hole across the street from the studio, tossed back a shot of Old Bushmills, and tried to figure out a way to come off as older. Or younger. Or taller. Oh well.

After Mark came home from filming *Star Wars*, he entertained Jan and me with stories about how privileged he felt to work with Alec Guinness, how funny Carrie Fisher was, what an adventure it was to shoot in the Tunisian desert, and how to "fight" with a light saber. (I learned from Mark just how far special effects had come since the days of our favorite FX pioneer, Ray Harryhausen.) As a science fiction fanboy himself,

Mark was one of the few people in the world who, early on, predicted that *Star Wars* was going to be an international smash.

By then, I was living by the adage that actors should act. I'd seen too many of my New York and Academy of Dramatic Art friends—many of whom were far more talented than me—fall through the cracks and fail because they refused to take roles that required them to leave Manhattan, or that they considered to be beneath them. I'm not saying I accepted each and every job that came my way, but I was probably somewhat less discerning than my East Coast friends and old pals from the ADA. It's great to be recognized, but the fact is I'm just a character actor, a working stiff, and the majority of the time, if somebody wants to hire me, I'm there.

IN 1976, I WENT up for the second male lead, a roadie named Bobbie Ritchie, in the remake of the classic film *A Star Is Born*. My main competition for the part was, you guessed it, Gary Busey. Gary's a real musician, so he logically got the role, and I had no problem with that. But the casting people liked me well enough that they threw me a bone in the form of a small but memorable part. I played the obnoxious redneck fan of the film's costar, Kris Kristofferson. During my big scene, my character pestered Kris's character to give me an autograph while the female lead, Barbra Streisand, was trying to sing a pretty little song. Kris refused, and I wouldn't take no for an answer, so the whole thing turned into a big old fight, but, unlike my fight scene in *Stay Hungry*, I didn't get whacked in the balls.

The morning of my scene, I sauntered over to a backstage mirror to check my hair—I was going for a white-trash rockabilly look—and picked up one of the fancy hairbrushes by the mirror. While I was trying to get my do to curl over my forehead just right, I noticed in the mirror one of the makeup girls staring at me with alarm. I felt a presence behind me; I turned around, and there she was, in all her superstar glory, Ms. Streisand herself, a sly smile on her face. Turned out I was grooming myself with La Streisand's personal on-set antique makeup kit. Thank God I hadn't used the brush yet. I gently placed it back on its tray and skulked away.

We filmed in Pasadena, and my portion of the shoot was going smoothly . . . more or less. Kristofferson had just gotten into acting, and he was working hard to make his character as realistic as possible, the result being that in our fight scene, he actually *fought*. During one of the takes, he clipped me on the nose pretty good, and I actually saw stars. He felt awful about it and apologized profusely. I think Kris thought I was a stuntman, and he was allowed to make full contact with stuntmen. Wrong. I was a working stiff, and working stiffs don't like knuckle sandwiches. (Getting punched by big stars turned out to be a theme in my early career. At the same studio, two years later, I'd get poked in the nose by Richard Gere during the filming of a drama called *Bloodbrothers*. I was wearing some disco platform boots, and when Richard knocked me backward, I aggravated an old ankle injury, which taught me that regardless of what the director or costume designer says, forsake vanity and accuracy and always wear sensible shoes.)

The budget for *A Star Is Born* was close to $6 million, which, in 1976, was exorbitant. For the first time I had a trailer dressing room all to myself, complete with my very own color television. The catering was gourmet, and I haven't eaten as well on a movie since. I'd arrived.

Now, who would be the most logical person to work with after the incomparable Barbra Streisand? Maybe Robert Redford? Nah. Possibly Dustin Hoffman? No way. How about the guy who directed *The Texas Chain Saw Massacre*?

Hell, yeah. Now we're talking.

IN 1974, A THIRTY-ONE-YEAR-OLD director named Tobe Hooper released his second film, a graphic slasher movie called *The Texas Chain Saw Massacre*. The title pretty much sums it up—a bunch of Texas teenagers get tormented by a chainsaw-wielding hitchhiker and his merry band of murderers—and it became an immediate cult classic, so much so that it both informed the style of and established genre elements that would be ripped off by generations of future filmmakers. Three years later came Tobe's follow-up, *Death Watch*, which was eventually renamed *Eaten Alive,* and what a crazy cast: Oscar nominees Carolyn Jones and Stuart Whitman; Audrey Hepburn's husband, Mel Ferrer; veteran TV and film character actor Neville Brand; a Brian De Palma regular named William Finley; and former Teenage Drama Workshop stalwart Robert Englund.

The first time I walked on the soundstage, I was blown away

by the set: an old Victorian farmhouse surrounded by tumble-weeds, cacti, ominous dead trees, frantic caged animals, and an old convertible Caddy El Dorado parked by the veranda, all enveloped by a low-hanging Hollywood fog. Truly a frightening atmosphere. In the midst of all this sat my long-haired, shaggy-bearded director, Mr. Hooper. I love Tobe, in part because he's an original. He's an intellectual with a professor's vocabulary, which he growls at you with his bark of a voice. He was never without a thin brown Sherman cigarette in his hand and was always excited to converse about anything at length: history, literature, movies, rock and roll, you name it.

Having never done a horror film, I had no idea what to expect; I certainly didn't anticipate its being so much fun. (Okay, wrestling a rubber alligator in freezing water wasn't a blast, but what're you gonna do?) And for the record, in the Japanese version of the film, that is *not* my penis.

Working with Tobe whetted my appetite for more horror flicks, but first, it was time to try out for a western, albeit a contemporary one. The film: *The Last of the Cowboys*. The stars: Henry Fonda and Susan Sarandon. I needed to beat out Michael Sacks, the Golden Globe–nominated star of *Slaughterhouse-Five*, for the role of Beebo Crozier.

The auditions were at a dingy little office out in North Hollywood. I went in for my final callback, and who walks in while I'm sitting on the floor in the waiting room? Ms. Sarandon, with her Bette Davis eyes. She smiled at me, said hello, then leaned over and gave me a tender kiss on the cheek. I knew right then she was in my corner, and I had a legitimate chance at getting the part. I aced my final audition and was almost in. I only had one more obstacle: Henry Fonda. Since most of Henry's scenes were with Beebo, he had final approval of who got the role.

The next morning, I was sent to Henry's estate in Bel-Air. The 1920s Spanish hacienda had polished tile floors and an impressive collection of art hanging on the walls. I followed his wife, Shirlee, down a long hall to a study in the back, where on the table sat a pitcher of fresh lemonade, and a copy of the *Cowboys* script marked up in different-colored pencils. Then in walks the man himself, the great Henry Fonda, wearing a beekeeper's outfit. He took off the mesh bonnet, put some fresh honey on the table, then started to gently grill me. After about an hour, he smiled, stuck out his hand, and said, "Robert, I look forward to working with you." I don't even remember retracing my steps through the corridors of the great actor's home; I was just so relieved to have won him over.

Despite the high-powered cast, this was an independent movie with a low budget, so it was back to sharing a small Winnebago with two other people. Fortunately, those people were Henry and Shirlee Fonda. Since I'd recently become a classic-film buff, all I wanted to do was quiz Henry in depth about his illustrious career in Hollywood. *Tell me about the making of* The Grapes of Wrath. . . . *What was it like shooting with Hitchcock on* The Wrong Man? . . . *Was it fun working on* The Lady Eve, *that screwball comedy where you play a geeky guy, and I need to know because that's my favorite movie of yours.* . . . But I bit my tongue and reined myself in. He was carrying the entire film, and since he'd just had an operation, I figured he needed his energy, so I gave him his space and permitted myself only one pestering question per day. Well, maybe two.

One afternoon, I was passionately prattling on and on about a play I'd done back at the Meadow Brook Theatre, and at that moment Henry—who considered himself first and foremost a man of the theater—totally warmed up to me. Then the floodgates opened. He told me about the first time he met Jimmy Stewart, and how charismatic a young Bette Davis was, and how when Barbara Stanwyck started filming a movie, she made it a point to learn everybody's name in the cast and crew. It was a steady diet of Old Hollywood tales, and I devoured every word of it. Hollywood history from the horse's mouth.

Henry liked to bitch about the truck situation. His character drove an eighteen-wheeler throughout most of the movie, so several weeks before shooting began, he took about a dozen lessons. Turned out that for insurance reasons, the producers wouldn't let him drive the truck. He was serious about preparing for a role, so when he realized he'd wasted all that time in truck-driving class, it pissed him off.

This movie was a turning point in my career. Knowing I was accepted by the likes of Susan Sarandon and Henry Fonda gave me another shot of confidence that would fuel me through the countless interviews, auditions, and rejections that lay ahead.

SOON AFTER *THE LAST OF THE COWBOYS* wrapped, Jan and I moved out of our Schindler apartment, and we rented our own place by the beach in Santa Monica, smack in the middle of what the surfers and skateboarders referred to as Dogtown.

Our upstairs neighbor was comic actor Andy Kaufman, and he was every bit as eccentric as you might imagine.

Most every Saturday night, Jan and I invited friends over for pizza, beer, a little weed, and some *Saturday Night Live.* (This was during the show's early glory days, when people's weekend plans revolved around staying home to watch *SNL.*) Andy had been on the first episode in 1975, and to us he was synonymous with the show. One night in 1976, we were hooting and hollering at a particularly funny sketch, after which, during a commercial break, we heard a knock at the door. I opened up, and there stood Andy. He spoke in the timid, foreign voice that was one of the signature shticks of his act: "Excuse me, please, could you not be making so much noise, please? Tenk you veddy much." We all knew that Andy was from Long Island, and the voice was a put-on. Funny guy, still in character.

I said, "Andy! Come in! We love you!" I didn't think the pervasive scent of marijuana would bother him too much.

He shook his head. "Please to just keep it down. Tenk you veddy much." To this day, I don't know if he was messing with us, or if he was practicing. Maybe he had an audition the next day and he was annoyed that we'd awakened him. Or maybe he was testing his "foreign man" character on a captive audience. Or maybe Andy Kaufman was just a strange, strange guy.

Several months later, I was auditioning for a little television show called *Taxi.* I was up for the role of Bobby, the vain actor who drives a cab to supplement his income while he tries to make it in New York City. I had a couple of callbacks, and the casting people decided I wasn't right for Bobby, but they saw something in me and asked me to read for the role of Latka, the sweet mechanic from a country of unknown origin. After a quick skim of the script, I asked, "So what do you guys want here, an Andy Kaufman impression?"

They collectively shrugged and asked, "Who?" I don't think they knew who Andy Kaufman was. I gave it my best shot. Next thing I knew, Andy had the part. Me and my big mouth.

IN 1977, MY FRIENDLY nemesis Gary Busey and I both auditioned for a surfing movie called *Big Wednesday;* this time, however, we weren't up for the same part. Fortunately for Gary, he got the role he'd tried out for. Unfortunately for me, I didn't, which stung, because I was an honest-to-goodness surfer. But as was the case with *A Star Is Born,* again the casting folks at Warner Bros. threw me a bone. It turned out to be a lucrative bone because even though I only had a featured part, the production went over schedule, so I ended up taking home more money for this small role than I had for any of my starring roles to date. Plus I got to hang out on location at one of the most beautiful beaches in all of California. All things considered, there was nothing to complain about. (There's that famous saying in the theater, "There are no small roles, only small actors." In Hollywood, that axiom could be changed to "There are sometimes small roles that lead to big paychecks.")

Our director, John Milius, also wrote the movie, and the rule on the set was that you shouldn't fuck with a single word or change even a comma in the script if you knew what was good for you. I could respect that because Milius had written one of my favorite flicks, *The Wind and the Lion,* as well as *Dirty Harry,* and Robert Shaw's monologue about the torpedoed USS *Indianapolis* shark-feeding frenzy in *Jaws,* so who was I to start improvising?

But I did.

Near the end of the film, in a scene where one of the leads, played by *The Greatest American Hero,* William Katt, is headed off to fight in Vietnam, I improvised the line "Stay casual, Barlow," which was my interpretation of how a surfer would say "Keep your head down." Milius didn't flip out; for that matter he left it in, and it became one of the most memorable, oft-quoted lines in the movie. To this day surfers still shout "Stay casual!" when they see me at the beach.

TV Movies of the Week often get a bad rap—we've all suffered through a disease-of-the-moment chick flick—but I've appeared in over a dozen MOWs, most of which were quality fare with stellar casts. In 1979, I did one for CBS called *Mind over Murder,* directed by Ivan Nagy, a Hungarian director whose name turned up some fifteen-odd years later in the Heidi Fleiss scandal. One of the stars of the movie, Andrew Prine, played a serial killer who was pursued by detectives through a dreamlike ESP connection. Andrew had shaved his head for the role, giving him a distinctive, haunting look. (Sound familiar?) Andrew was so effective in that dark little TV movie that I believe I subconsciously drew on his work when I began my own filmic killing spree five years later.

But before I drew first blood as Freddy, I had to endure a *Galaxy of Terror.*

* * *

CUT TO 1981. WITH an impending actors' strike, I was taking any job I could get: bit parts on *Charlie's Angels, Alice, CHiPS*, and a low-budget horror film called *Dead and Buried*, anything to gather myself some acorns for what might turn out to be a long winter.

At that moment, for us actors, timing was everything. If a film or television show went into production before the strike, it wouldn't have to shut down, but if a project hadn't started shooting, regardless of how far along in preproduction it was, it had to be shelved until an agreement was reached.

Fortunately, an old inspiration, and one of the busiest producers in Hollywood, came to my rescue with a role.

For his movie *Galaxy of Terror*, B-movie impresario Roger Corman assembled one of the most eccentric ensembles I've ever worked with. We're talking Ray Walston (Judge Bone from *Picket Fences*); Erin Moran (Joanie from *Happy Days*); Grace Zabriskie (Sarah Palmer from *Twin Peaks*, Mrs. Ross from *Seinfeld*, and Lois from *Big Love*); Zalman King (writer of *Nine ½ Weeks*, and creator of *Red Shoe Diaries*); and yours truly.

It was certainly great to be working for Corman from a creative perspective, but—how do I put this politely?—well, let's just say, Roger's a bit of a tightwad. We're talking killer hours, and catering that consisted of peanut-butter-and-jelly sandwiches for breakfast, lunch, and dinner. My dressing room was fashioned from two bookended canvas flats, furnished with a white plastic chair, and a single bent nail to hang my clothes on. It's not the most glamorous way to make a movie, but you have to give the guy credit: as of this writing, he's been making films for fifty-five years and has executive-produced and/or produced and/or directed and/or written something like four hundred movies. Roger also has a remarkable eye for talent; he was an early supporter of such stars-to-be as Jack Nicholson, Barbara Hershey, and Francis Ford Coppola, just to name a few. Point being, if you ever have the opportunity to appear in a Roger Corman movie, jump on it no matter how shitty your salary might be, because that is one man in Hollywood who knows what the hell he's doing.

I also wanted to work with Roger for another reason: *Boxcar Bertha*, the Scorsese-helmed movie Roger produced, was what helped inspire me to leave the theater for the movies in the first place. I'd come full circle. The gig was meant to be.

We shot at Roger's new studio/backlot in Venice Beach, a once dicey area that was just beginning to gentrify; out with the hippies, in with the yuppies. My first day on set, I was really impressed. We had zero budget, but the production design looked as if it cost a million bucks. I noticed that the art director's office was right across the hall from my lean-to dressing room, so I wandered over and saw a guy with a long blond ponytail sitting on the floor, surrounded by rough blueprints and really cool drawings of the monster who would be terrorizing our cast over the next couple of weeks.

A few days later I stole one of the crumpled illustrations from the art department floor and pinned it up in my dressing room. I later learned the name of the young ponytailed guy on the floor: James Cameron. Considering what James went on to direct—*Titanic, The Terminator, True Lies*—I wish I'd kept those discarded drawings.

James wasn't even thirty years old and was already a genius.

For the spaceship that flew all around the infamous galaxy of terror, he took his buck-ninety-nine budget (or however little Roger gave him to work with) and turned the spacecraft's hexagon-shaped corridor into a set worthy of something from *2001: A Space Odyssey* using only milk crates and Styrofoam take-out containers that began their lives as the home of a McDonald's Big Mac. The crates were hanging from the ceiling, and the light shone through the grates, creating an eerie dappled effect. The hamburger boxes were stapled open on the walls, completing the design. It's not an exaggeration to say that dozens of movies had budgets fifty times greater than ours that didn't look nearly as good.

During the shoot, a rumor started going around that Roger had rented out the set to a German watch company for a commercial shoot and they paid him enough to make back the entire budget of *Galaxy of Terror* and then some. We never found out if that was true, but if it wasn't, it should've been, because that is Roger Corman in a nutshell.

THE FOLLOWING YEAR, IT was off to the Philippines for a Vietnam movie with the awkward title of *Don't Cry, It's Only Thunder*. This was my first time shooting outside the USA, and my first trip to the Far East, so a couple weeks before I was scheduled to catch my plane, I went to see the studio-appointed doctor so I could schedule my series of malaria inoculations. (If Roger Corman did a movie over in Asia, I'm pretty certain he would've made us pay for our own shots.) I was then flown to

Manila and put up in a five-star hotel for a whole two weeks before filming started, so I could get acclimated to the time change, the punishing humidity, and the culture shock.

We soon shifted locations to an air force base in a province up north. I reluctantly checked out of my fancy Manila digs and naively hoped my next lodging would be as plush. The military folks had reserved a few rooms for us near the officers' quarters on the base, and they were homey, clean, safe, and comfortable. Unfortunately, there was only enough housing for the director and the two stars. We costarring types were bivouacked at a brothel off-base.

The rooms at our cathouse were spartan—especially compared to where we'd just come from—but on the plus side, a twenty-four-hour restaurant/bar was on the premises, and we were surrounded by jungle and roaming bison. Each room was furnished with a simple bed, a chair, a lizard on the wall, a portable black-and-white TV, and a prostitute. And you couldn't refuse. She was part of the deal. You get a room, you get a whore.

My fellow costar James Whitmore Jr. was staying across the hall. Our first night there, he knocked on my door. I let him in, and he glanced at my hooker and whispered, "I need a favor."

"What?"

"Switch girls with me."

"Excuse me?"

"I like yours. We hit it off in the bar last night. Come on, take mine. She's cute."

I wasn't intending to avail myself of my hooker's services anyway, so I said, "Sure. But you have to tell them it was your idea. I don't want to hurt anybody's feelings here."

Everywhere I went—which wasn't too far; I didn't stray much farther than a three-block radius of the whorehouse—my prostitute came with me. She was a nice enough girl, but she had one strange quirk: whenever we were in the bar, she ordered several double screwdrivers but never got drunk. I had to pay for them out of my per diem, and, man, were those things expensive.

I mentioned it to James, and he whispered, "She's not ordering screwdrivers. That's just orange juice."

"That's a hell of a lot of orange juice."

"She's not drinking it. Watch her carefully. She just pretends to drink it, then she hides the glass under the table and pours it into a baby bottle. She's taking it home for her kids." That broke my heart. After I found that out, I was happy to let her tag along with me, to buy her a meal or two, as well as all the OJ she wanted. I had become an accidental ambassador of American goodwill at a house of ill repute far from home.

None of my recent locales—Oakland, Michigan; New York City; Statesboro, Georgia; Birmingham, Alabama; or, for that matter, Hollywood—had prepared me for my overseas adventures in the Philippines. Now I was a seasoned veteran of exotic foreign locations ready for anything that show business could throw my way.

CHAPTER 5

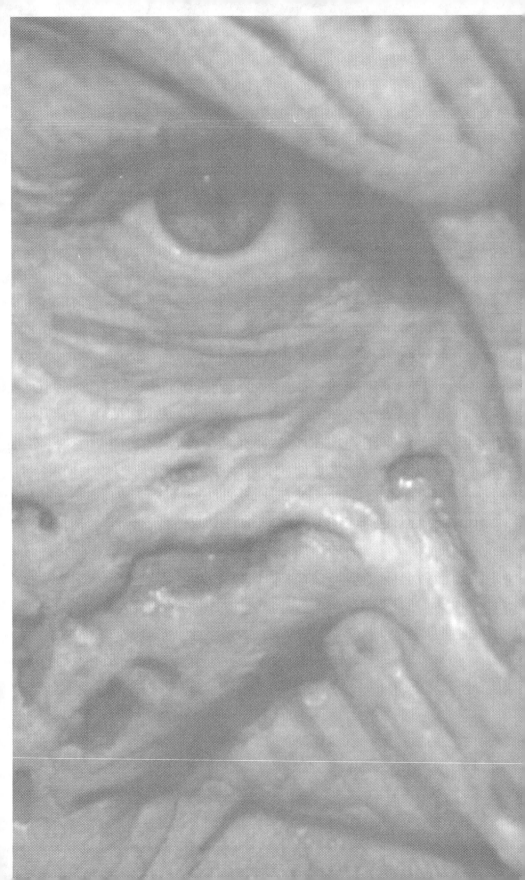

NIGHTMARE #5:

I'm backstage in a vaguely familiar old theater. A Shakespearean tragedy is being performed onstage under the lights. . . . I've forgotten my lines. . . . I feel pressure in my chest, a shortness of breath, I am pacing back and forth in the wings and looking for something I've lost. . . . I can't find a script I've hidden that contains my dialogue. . . . I hear my cue from onstage. . . . I search everywhere for the script and can't find it. . . . Then the dream starts all over again, repeats itself. . . . I have this nightmare once a year, without fail, and, man, does it suck.

*J*AN BEGAN WRITING AND PERFORMING WITH AN improvisational comedy group in L.A., and before long they got good, *real* good, so good that they started making regular appearances on NBC's *Don Kirshner's Rock Concert*, a pre-MTV promotional-rock-video-clip variety show that came on right after *Saturday Night Live*. Her comedy group, the Village Idiots, was loaded with talent, and one of their go-to guys was an energetic kid with a quick wit and a receding hairline named Michael Douglas. Not wanting to compete with *that* Michael Douglas, he changed his name to Michael Keaton and, within two years, was one of Hollywood's biggest box-office draws. (Attention sci-fi fans: when Michael left, he was replaced by Peter Jurasik, who later went on to star in *Babylon 5*.) When the Village Idiots gigged at the local comedy clubs, we'd run into unknown, hilarious performers such as Jim Carrey, Robin Williams, Sandra Bernhard, and Comedy Store emcee David Letterman, who introduced Jan to her eventual favorite cocktail, J.B. on the rocks.

Horny-pigeon performances notwithstanding, I wasn't trained as an improvisational actor, and I picked up a lot about making people laugh just by being a fly on the wall during the free-wheeling sessions in those late-night clubs, watching a generation of new talent incubate on those stages in the wee hours. It also nudged me closer to being an official cog in the New

Hollywood machine. For better or worse, the stage, my classical training, and Lee Strasberg's class were becoming a somewhat distant, albeit beloved, memory.

Whether I knew it—or admitted it—Jan's gang affected my acting. Despite my "Stay casual, Barlow" moment during *Big Wednesday*, I generally stuck to what was written on the page, but Michael's, Jan's, and Peter's ease with improv—and their joy when they came up with stuff on the spot that *worked*— gave me the confidence to play with my scripts a little, both on the set and at auditions. I realized that some TV-audition material wasn't exactly Shakespeare; it wasn't written in stone. Plus I'd done enough solid work, and I had a good enough reputation, that I wasn't concerned about getting fired for saying, "Hey, fella, the 1950s called, and they want their leather jacket back," rather than "That outfit isn't exactly your best look." When I was at ADA, it was drilled into us: *The text is sacred. Anything you need, you can find in the text. Serve the writer, then the director, then yourself. The play's the thing.* I don't think Robin Williams always played by those rules and he did okay, so if a little improv was good enough for Mork, it was good enough for me.

IN 1983, I MET Gregory Harrison of *Trapper John, M.D.* fame while costarring on a TV movie called *The Fighter*. Greg, who was also a stage actor, had just finished a sold-out run in downtown L.A. in a play called *The Hasty Heart* and was able to parlay that success into producing the play *Journey's End*, which ended up being filmed by a fledgling entertainment company called Home Box Office. I hadn't done any stage work for a while, so Jan dared me to audition for it. I was asked to do a part and I'm glad I did because I had the opportunity to work alongside an improvisational comedic genius named George Wendt. George had replaced John Belushi at Second City back in Chicago, and acting with him made me feel as though I was six degrees of separation from the original *SNL* cast. The play was a huge hit and attracted a whole flock of agents, producers, and casting directors to our postage-stamp–size stage adjacent to Paramount Studios.

(A side note: during the run of *Journey's End,* George auditioned for the television show that would all but define his career, *Cheers.* When he was told the part of Norm was his for the taking, he was on the fence between accepting that role or another pilot he had been offered. When, over a couple of beers, he asked me my opinion, I said, "You know what? I loved Ted Danson in that movie *The Onion Field.* I think you oughta do that *Cheers* show." The rest is television history.)

KENNETH JOHNSON HAD BEEN working on TV dramas since the late 1960s, and was best known for producing and writing many episodes of *The Six Million Dollar Man,* and creating its spin-off, *The Bionic Woman.* At that moment, his main task was executive-producing the show he'd created in 1978, *The Incredible Hulk.* He clearly had an affinity for one-hour science-fiction-oriented dramas, and he graduated to the long-form miniseries with a script about a bunch of aliens who come to Earth looking and acting like the nicest human beings you'd ever want to meet. Unfortunately for the population of our fine planet, these aliens are actually evil lizards that want to pillage Earth for its natural resources (humans!) to help resuscitate their dying home planet. In the midst of this mayhem, we meet a kind, lovable alien named Willie, the show's comic relief, who becomes a hero of sorts—the perfect part for a kind, lovable guy such as me. The miniseries was called *V*.

Thanks to my casting friends at Warner Bros., I was asked to read for the role, and going in, I found that my recent exposure to improv comedy, combined with six months of stage work in *Journey's End*, helped loosen me up for my audition. The reading was held on the Warner's backlot, and by that time I'd done so much work at Warner Bros. that I didn't even have to show my ID to the studio security guard. After I parked, I went up to Ken Johnson's office. After a few minutes of small talk, I asked if he had any specific notes as to how I should play Willie. He thought for a moment, then looked up, scratched his beard, and said, "Okay. Two words. Gene Wilder."

I consider Gene Wilder one of the great comic actors of his generation. I'd idolized him since 1967, when I saw him steal a scene from Warren Beatty from the backseat of Clyde Barrow's getaway car in *Bonnie and Clyde*, and of course he was brilliant in *The Producers*, not to mention that *Young Frankenstein* is one of my favorite movies. So when Ken suggested that I play this shy, sweet, confused alien-cum-lizard-cum-human with a dash of Wilder thrown in, not only was I thrilled that Ken and I shared a comic hero, but I knew exactly what he was looking for. He wanted awkward pauses, a sense of surprise, and offbeat comedy timing. I channeled Gene. And it worked.

A property of NBC, *V* was a big-budget project, the kind of budget that would make Roger Corman weep with envy. (Actually, if Roger ever got *V* money, he'd have used it to make twenty-eight films and build a new studio, and he'd still have enough money left over to spend a month at a château in the south of France.) Thus plenty of money was around to afford me state-of-the-art Hollywood-studio makeup special effects, circa 1983. But that art was not very advanced.

For example, in one scene Willie's face had to look as if it were burned by ice, so the makeup crew got a bunch of green grapes, cut them in half, laid me on my back, affixed the fruit to my cheeks, nose, and forehead, then dripped melted paraffin all over my face. Now the only thing I knew about paraffin was that back in my younger days I would grab a handful of it, toss it into a pot, heat it over the stove, then drip the hot liquid wax on the deck of my surfboard so I'd have better traction in the surf; I had no idea the stuff could serve any cinematic purpose. But the makeup crew knew what they were doing. My face looked blistered and frozen. Their low-tech recipe worked. For the first time—but certainly not the last—I felt like a modern-day Lon Chaney.

However, that wasn't the toughest makeup application I had to endure as Willie. In a later chapter of *V*, Willie had to undergo what could only be described as an alien allergy test, and to display his lizard scales in their full glory, I had to be fitted with a big, bulky back piece. One weekend, on a day off from shooting, I went to the makeup lab on the Warner Bros. lot—which wasn't anywhere near as sophisticated as it would become a few years later, when artists such as Rick Baker of *Men in Black* and *The Nutty Professor* fame would rule the makeup special effects world.

The old-school makeup technicians, who were all dressed in white lab coats and resembled the researchers from those old Volkswagen commercials, ordered me to lie facedown on a cold stainless-steel table. All these guys were older and jaded, except for one of the apprentices, a young man with long hair, headphones, and a positive, eager attitude. If not for his joking with me through the process, I might've jumped off that coroner's slab, grabbed Jan and my surfboard, and gone to the beach.

KEN JOHNSON HAD CONCEIVED *V* as an allegory for the occupation of Europe and the survival of the Jews in the ghettos during World War II. The alien's logo had a Nazi-like vibe, and the uniforms and sunglasses had a storm-trooper ethos about them, plus many of the actors who were cast as the aliens had a Germanic, Teutonic look, so the message wasn't exactly subtle, but it gave the whole project some gravitas.

The actress who played our Anne Frank was Dominique Dunne, the daughter of journalist and author Dominick Dunne, and sister of actor Griffin Dunne. Dominique had played the teenage daughter in *Poltergeist*, a superb horror thriller directed by my old pal Tobe Hooper. Soon after *Poltergeist*, she met an up-and-coming chef named John Thomas Sweeney. She and Sweeney fell in love and moved in together, and almost immediately John regularly abused the hell out of her. Dominique

dumped Sweeney, and after she refused to reconcile, he stran-
gled her in her own driveway. She went into a coma and died
five days later. Sweeney served a grand total of two and a half
years. (Nice penal system, right?) Dominique's senseless death
saddened all who knew and worked with her on *V*, and the tragedy brought the entire production team closer together. You've
probably heard actors say time and again that "everybody on
this movie became just like a family," and most of the time
that's just lip service. In our case, we did support one another
both professionally and personally, just as a real family would.
We all believed in the project and wanted it to be the best it
could be, so we soldiered on through our grief and produced
what everybody felt was some pretty good work.

The ad campaign for *V* was the most imaginative and sub-
versive since *Rosemary's Baby* in 1968, fifteen years earlier.
For that campaign, the studio had hired an army of people to
stencil baby carriages on the sidewalks of busy city intersec-
tions, and in front of movie theaters. They also put up billboards that said PRAY FOR ROSEMARY'S BABY, without explaining
who Rosemary was, and why we should talk to God about her
brat. *Rosemary's Baby* is a certified classic now and would
probably have made its mark strictly on its merits, but that
alternative campaign pushed it over the edge.

Somebody in the NBC advertising department must've
paid attention. They blanketed the country with billboards
that looked as if graffiti artists had defaced them; all you saw
was a giant, spray-painted red *V*. The general reaction to the
billboards was "What the fuck is that?" which is just about
the best publicity one could hope for. NBC also came up with a
terrific batch of commercials that made your television screen

get all fuzzy and staticky, as if the station had gone off the air. Then, as if it suddenly had a mind of its own, the picture would click back on and the screen filled with the warning THE VISITORS ARE COMING. (*V*, as people were starting to realize, was an abbreviation for "Visitors.") The hype was imaginative and pervasive, and with only three major networks back then, it entered the collective consciousness of the nation's TV viewers—especially sci-fi-starved fans—which boded well for heavy media coverage and big ratings.

It worked. *V* became a cultural phenomenon, not just in the United States, but throughout the world. It was one of the highest rated miniseries in television history, so almost overnight I started getting recognized on the street. None of the films or TV movies I'd appeared in before had had anywhere near the visibility that *V* did, and suddenly I was on the pop-culture radar. I immediately learned that in terms of recognition, television makes far more of an impact than film. TV fans don't have to pay to see you, plus you're right there in their living rooms night after night, week after week, which means that it's all but guaranteed that at some point during the run of your series, somebody will ask you for an autograph while you're shaking off at a urinal.

MY LIFE AS A semi-anonymous character actor ceased to exist. It was my first bout with national celebrity, and it made those fallen nuns back in Cleveland who tracked me down backstage at *Godspell*, or the little kids who wanted Pinocchio's autograph at the Teenage Drama Workshop, seem like another lifetime. People bought me drinks at bars, and meals at restaurants, and I was constantly signing pictures of America's new favorite alien. Science fiction and horror fans are an intense, knowledgeable, loyal crowd, so I was besieged by fans with arcane questions about Willie, and his ability to straddle two worlds. My feeble answer was along the lines of "Uh . . . you should probably write to Ken Johnson. He'll know."

For the first time, I was getting fan mail . . . and lots of it, more than I could handle. As I discovered, it was more than Warner Bros./NBC TV could handle too. One afternoon during a break from shooting *V*, I went across the lot to visit a friend of mine who was guest-starring on the prime-time soap *Hotel*. The main set was the lobby of a grand hotel, complete with cubbyholes behind the reception desk, where the concierge could leave mail or messages for the guests. My friend pointed to the cubbies, which were filled with assorted envelopes, and said, "See that? They have to put prop letters in there, and the prop guys are using studio fan mail they found in the trash. A lot of it was addressed to Willie." (So if you wrote me a letter during my *V* years and I didn't answer it, you can blame the Warner Bros./NBC publicity department.)

For me, the timing of this show couldn't have been better. In the early eighties, few science fiction shows were on American network television; hard-core sci-fi nuts were watching either syndicated reruns of *Star Trek* on their local stations, or flipping over to PBS for *Doctor Who* marathons. This was a neglected demographic that we happily catered to. Sure, *V* was a fine show, and I'm still proud of it, but the mammoth size of our audience wasn't only about quality; it was also a happy synergy of timing and marketing. *V* filled a void, and luckily for me, Willie—a malaprop-spewing alien who is all about peace, love, and understanding—became one of the viewers' favorites. I too filled a void and became a sort of de facto Dr. Spock for the post–boomer generation.

I was invited to a number of science fiction festivals, and I had no idea what the hell they were about, although I suspected it was going to be a bunch of nerdy Trekkies. Would it involve simply signing autographs, or Q&A sessions, or would I have to do a few Willie impersonations? I quickly learned that the sci-fi subculture was evolving from isolated underground fanboys to hundreds of thousands of hard-core followers valued by the industry, and attention must be paid. The crossover popularity of Comic-Con was still several years away, but I had a front-row seat for the genesis. (Many of those aforementioned nerdy Trekkies now rule the world. They're game programmers and softwear designers and comic-book artists, and, of course, film and television executives. They embraced their Trekkie origins and unashamedly let their geek flag fly, and look where it got them.)

The miniseries was such a phenomenon, it was only logical that *V* became a full-blown weekly series. In the fine print of my contract, it read that *V* could be construed as either a miniseries or a TV movie, and if it was deemed to be a TV movie, it could also be construed as a pilot for a weekly series. Rather than dive into a weekly show, the network opted to do a longer miniseries—it would run ten hours rather than four—which sounded fine to me. My agent negotiated a deal that everybody was happy with, so when *V: The Final Battle* went into production in 1984, I'd be there.

But first came a hiatus, during which plenty of casting people contacted me. In one instance, I was up for literally every male role in *National Lampoon's Class Reunion*, probably the first serial-killer spoof in film history. *National Lampoon* had proved they could make a classic comedy with *Animal House*, so I wanted in. I was up for the killer, the hero, the jock, the nerd, every-fucking-body, and after half a dozen callbacks, I was certain I was going to attend that *Class Reunion*. Well, I was wrong. I got nothing. Nada. Zero. Bubkes. All those callbacks must have canceled each other out and done more harm than good, and after that I decided that it would take a hell of a lot to get me to ever go on a callback again.

I think the *Class Reunion* casting director, Annette Benson, might have felt funny about having me come back so many times to audition for so many parts and then end up empty-handed, so she called my agent, Joe Rice, and asked him if I'd consider a horror movie.

I had fond memories from *Eaten Alive* with Tobe Hooper, and *Galaxy of Terror* with Roger Corman, so I told Joe, "I had fun working on them in the past. I'd definitely consider it." Plus, I was beginning to feel a little typecast as Lizard Boy on *V,* and this might be an opportunity to remind audiences I had a darker side.

Joe said, "Terrific. Annette might just have something for you. There's a director she wants you to meet. Today."

So that afternoon, I hopped into my 1968, powder-blue Datsun 2000 convertible—she wasn't cherry but was a great car to zoom around L.A. in—and drove across town to speak with Annette about a little project called *A Nightmare on Elm Street,* written and directed by Wes Craven.

* * *

WES'S FIRST MOVIE, *LAST HOUSE ON THE LEFT*, was released in 1972, right when I moved back to California. A cross between Ingmar Bergman's *Virgin Spring* and a contemporary, no-holds-barred horror movie, *Last House on the Left* was about a couple of hot girls, a rock band called Bloodlust, some psychotic escaped prisoners, sex, rape, and, most disconcertingly, a blow job gone awry. (At the time of its release, I was on my rediscovering-classic-America-cinema kick, so it wasn't really on my radar.) Five years later, Wes made his second feature, another horror flick, called *The Hills Have Eyes*, for a grand total of $230,000. It made money hand over fist and achieved cult status. Wes could put asses in theater seats, scare the shit out of you, and turn a pretty penny, so it was little surprise that he'd become a legitimate Hollywood player.

My contemporaries and I saw Wes as more of a David Lynch type. I was a huge Lynch fan, in part because one of my favorite new wave/ska bars in L.A. played a loop of scenes from David's 1977 weird-a-thon *Eraserhead* for hours at a time on their tiny black-and-white television behind the bar. When the bartender got tired of hearing Jack Nance's wailing mutant baby, he would fire up bootleg videos of *The Hills Have Eyes* and *Last House on the Left*. After a couple of Bushmills, all three movies fused together in my subconscious. I wasn't exactly frightened—I looked at these movies less as horror films and more as art-house cinema—but I was creeped out nonetheless.

All those bizarre movie images were running through my mind as I parked in the lot of the building where the production office was located. So I sat in my little Datsun convertible for a minute, gathering my thoughts. I glanced in the rearview mirror and saw my tanned face staring back at me, not exactly the kind of face that would scare your average moviegoer. When I pushed back my long blond hair and noticed that my forehead wasn't as dark as the rest of my face, I came up with an idea.

I hopped out of the car, opened up the hood, pulled out the oil dipstick, touched it with my finger, then used the oil to slick my curly hair straight back. Then, remembering that my buddy Demetre habitually left his cigarette butts in my ashtray, I slid back into the front seat, licked my finger, poked around in the ashtray, and gently dabbed some ash under my eyes. Again, I checked myself out in the mirror; with a greased-back receding hairline and dark circles under my eyes, I no longer looked like a sun-kissed California surfer. Feeling far scarier, I headed to the audition.

I had no idea what Wes Craven looked like. Considering his movies and his thematically appropriate last name, I guessed he might be some kind of arty Goth guy, with pale skin, long hair, and dressed head to toe in black. I walked in the room and was introduced to a tall, slender gentleman with an articulate, charming demeanor, and a sartorial style that would make Ralph Lauren proud. Wes was one class act.

Now I tend to be a motormouth, but I consider myself a pretty good communicator, so I went into that office, shook hands with Wes, sat down, and prepared to launch into what I hoped would be a fascinating dissertation on the horror genre. But before I could utter a single syllable, Wes began speaking. Thank God I kept my big mouth shut, because the guy is a hypnotic storyteller, a mesmerizing raconteur with a wonderful sense of humor, and I was spellbound. In the midst of his story, when I was about to interrupt with what I thought might be a relevant observation, a bell went off in my head: *Robert, zip it and just listen. And look scary.*

How did I accomplish that? Simple: I didn't blink. I stared at Wes and did everything I could to keep my eyelids frozen, as if I were trying to win a staring contest. I'm not sure he noticed, because he kept right on talking, waxing poetically about how the concept for *A Nightmare on Elm Street* originated.

It all started back when he was a kid. Wes and his brother were home alone. When they were getting ready for bed, as Wes went to close the curtain in their bedroom, he glanced out the window and noticed a man walking slowly down the sidewalk, alone, wearing a misshapen hat. From Wes's perspective, the guy looked kinda dirty; he might've been a hobo. The man passed beneath a streetlight, stopped, snapped his head up, and stared directly at little Wes in the window. It scared the shit out of him, so he violently jerked the curtains shut and told his brother what he'd seen. A few minutes later, they gathered their courage to peek through the curtains again. The bum was still there, staring up at the window. They shut the curtains, then, after a while, tiptoed down the stairs and peered through the front-door peephole. The man was standing on the Cravens' front walkway, and the brothers were scarred for life. The seed for one of the most successful, iconic horror franchises in showbiz history had been planted.

Wes gave me a quick rundown of the film's plot, stressing that it would be a surreal, dark, suburban fairy tale, a contemporary myth, an urban legend in the spirit of an uncensored Brothers Grimm story. The horror would be embodied not by Rumpelstiltskin, but by a disfigured bogeyman who haunts the dreams of his victims. This nightmare-dwelling specter: Fred Krueger.

Whoever played Freddy was going to be stuck wearing a ton of special effects makeup, and Wes asked me if I thought I could handle it. I told him that between the theater and *V*, getting into the makeup chair was second nature to me. (I was only fibbing a bit.) As the interview drew to a close, I continued trying to stare at Wes without blinking, not wanting to break character. I really wanted the part now, but didn't think I was going to get it; hearing Wes describe Freddy in depth, I assumed that they wanted a big stunt guy for the role. And honestly, that's how I envisioned Freddy too; I didn't really believe a blond-haired surfer who was just over five feet ten could portray this dream stalker.

But apparently Wes Craven believed. Two days later, a message was on my answering machine: the role was mine. Robert Englund was going to be Freddy Krueger. They hadn't given me a single line of dialogue to read, so I don't know what cinched it for me. It might've been the whole not-blinking thing. It might've been that Annette went to bat for me because she felt bad for making me audition for every fucking part in *National Lampoon's Class Reunion*. It might've been the hair plastered to my skull and my dark, sunken eyes. It might've been that they thought my thin face, when covered with layers of FX makeup, would still look like a normal-size head. Or it might just be that Wes saw something in me that I didn't even know existed.

After we worked out all the legalities, it dawned on me what I might be in for. I liked Wes, but I was a little concerned. Despite the Ralph Lauren attire and professorial attitude, this was the guy who'd bloodied the screen with *Last House on the Left*, and somebody with that dark of an imagination might not be right in the head. I also knew that the makeup could be a challenge. But I embraced it, because a little bit of the Teenage Drama Workshop–era Robbie Englund was still in me, the kid who liked to put on false beards and fake noses, the fan who liked to leaf through the *Life* magazine coffee-table books with pictures of Lon Chaney, the Man of a Thousand Faces, in all his silent film FX makeup incarnations. Even though I was in my midthirties, I understood that *Nightmare* might be a chance to rediscover the imagination of my childhood, to plug into that creative innocence. Also, I remembered that Laurence Olivier liked to change his look with every role—e.g., experiment with makeup, wear a humpback, or walk with a limp—so I figured if it was good enough for Sir Larry, it was good enough for me.

A COUPLE WEEKS BEFORE we were to start shooting, I drove way out in the Valley, to the home studio of one David Miller. David was a young FX makeup artist who'd only been in the business a few years, but had already made a significant splash with his work on the ultimate music video, Michael Jackson's "Thriller." David's job that day was to make a cast of my head with liquid latex so he could use it to begin creating the mold to sculpt Freddy's face. To prep me for the day's work, he showed me some preliminary sketches of Freddy, and some medical textbooks with photos of burn victims. Ironically, I got nightmares from those graphic images.

Getting my head cast was just about as much fun as getting whacked in the nuts with a pool cue. First, they jammed straws up my nose. Next, my skin was lathered with Vaseline, then they basted my head, neck, and shoulders with a cold goop called alginate. As the goop began to solidify, the makeup crew covered it with strips of wet plaster bandages to form a helmet. (I thought I was playing Freddy Krueger, not the fucking Mummy.) As the goop hardened it got hotter and hotter, trapping me in my own hellish sauna. Then, blind and practically deaf, hyperventilating through straws, I heard the muffled whine of a chain saw. (First the Mummy, now Leatherface? What was I getting into?) After they surgically sawed the helmet in half, David told me to lean forward, wrinkle my face, and gently retract my head from the mold. And there, imprinted in the plaster shell, was a perfect negative of my facial features. This would now be used as a mold to cast a bust of me that David would transform into Freddy Krueger.

Wes and Bob Shaye, the head of New Line Cinema, who was producing *A Nightmare on Elm Street*, joined me on my second trip to David's place to check the progress of the makeup. The fourteen pieces of the Freddy face needed to be colored (they were still in their pale pink powdered-latex condition) and assembled on my neck, ears, nose, lips, cheeks, forehead, and all the way down to my chest. It was like a huge Freddy Krueger puzzle. Once all the pieces were glued to my face with medical adhesive—the stuff used for colostomy bags—the cohesive mask needed to be painted. When the coloring was complete, Freddy emerged. As a finishing touch, David rubbed K-Y jelly onto the makeup so Freddy would seem to be covered with oozing, suppurating, pus-filled burn wounds. Mmm, yummy, lunchtime.

Wes and Bob wanted Freddy to have thin flaps of translucent flesh peeling from his face. Wes knew it would be difficult for continuity—think about how hard it would be to replicate a penny-size piece of skin hanging from my chin day after day—but he loved the image and gave it a try. He quickly realized that wrangling little pieces of latex flesh consumed too much time and opened a can of continuity worms. So, much to Bob's disappointment, the idea was bagged.

The first time I had the finished version of the Freddy makeup on—which took over three hours to apply—I realized that to activate the mask, to bring Freddy to life, I'd need to animate my own face more than I had in any other acting job before . . . well, except for maybe when I mugged my way through that Molière play in Detroit. To make the Krueger grimace work, and to allow my discolored teeth to be visible, I had to exaggerate. We also concluded that it would be effective if I kept the face passive sometimes and just exploited my eyes; if shot from the right angle, a fixed stare, a slow blink, or a malicious glare could be just as frightening as animated anger.

Wes had a concept for wardrobe, but was happy to turn its execution over to Team *Nightmare*. In the original script, he described Freddy's claw glove in great detail, and a mechanical special effects designer named Jim Doyle, and his assistant, Lou Carlucci, realized Wes's vision. (Initially, the claw was unwieldy and difficult to maneuver, and I used to wear it around the set so I could practice moving it naturally. My favorite thing to do was go over to the craft services table and spear a cocktail weenie or a cheese puff, then eat it right off the razor.)

Remembering the lesson I'd learned about sensible shoes during the filming of *Bloodbrothers*, I wore comfortable, broken-in work boots with thick heels, to give myself some extra height. Freddy's pants were described simply as work pants, and Wes decided that it would be appropriate for Freddy to wear neutral brown slacks covered with oil stains. After a week of greasy thighs at the end of each day, I put the kibosh on the daily lube job by the wardrobe girls.

Freddy's red-and-green-striped sweater was pure Wes; my contribution was the suggestion to fray it around the collar and the wrists. I asked that it not be as baggy as Wes had initially wanted because a tighter fit made for a stronger, more recognizable silhouette for Freddy. Wes never explained why he chose the colors red and green; my guess was that those two colors strobe on-screen, which is kind of nauseating, like the effect from 3-D glasses. It certainly had nothing to do with Christmas.

Then there was the hat, Freddy's venerable fedora. The day before shooting, I was in full makeup standing in a tiny room at the studio while David applied final touch-ups. Wes and Bob were in the room with us, parked on a cheap futon, throwing in their two cents' worth, making sure that Freddy was Just Right. Bob was still arguing for the flaps of flesh on Freddy's face, and our director of photography, Jacques Haitkin, was in Bob's camp, and Wes, ever the pragmatist, was reminding them that continuity would be a bitch. I was hot and tired, so I didn't give a shit.

On the floor of the small room sat a huge box of hats that I figured the wardrobe people had stuck in there just to get out of everybody's way. That wasn't the case: with shooting only one day away, everybody was panicked and had started second-guessing the hat choice for Freddy. So Bob and Wes made me plow through this entire box and try on hat after hat after hat, the worst of which was a 1930s-era hat that made me look as though I should be selling newspapers on a street corner during the Depression. I told them, "I swear if you guys make me wear this one, I'm getting on camera and saying, 'Extra! Extra! Read all about it! The villain from *A Nightmare on Elm Street* is wearing a stupid fucking hat!'"

I remembered my albino contact lens debacle from *Buster and Billie*, so I said, "Wes, the fedora was in the original script. I like it, and you dreamed it up, so why change it? And besides, it kind of reminds me of Lamont Cranston's slouch hat in *The Shadow*. 'Who knows what evil lurks in the hearts of men? Freddy Krueger knows.' Y'know?" Then I put on the fedora and tipped my hat to them a couple of times, demonstrating to Bob, Wes, and Jacques the advantage of the hat with different lighting, how it could hide Freddy's face and also reveal his scarred baldness in all its glorious naked horror. Then I put the hat on and pointed to my shadow on the wall: "Check out that silhouette." I believed in the hat, so I fought for it and, fortunately, won the battle. The fedora would become integral to Freddy's signature look.

A COUPLE WEEKS PRIOR, way deep down, on a gut level—while I was sitting in that fucking barber's chair in David Miller's garage studio, the kind of chair that I'd eventually spend hundreds of hours in—I knew that we'd come up with something special, something more than just a mere monster, and that even though I'd never done anything like this in my career, I'd be able to physicalize this character to a T and make it work. I didn't know that the child killer whom Wes, David, and I brought to life would become a pop-culture icon and survive for twenty-five years, but if you'd told me that would be the case, I wouldn't have been completely surprised.

After David tweaked the makeup to his satisfaction, I stared in the mirror and started messing around with different voices for Freddy; I could've tried to figure out something on my own, but it was far easier when I could stare at the Krueger face. I came up with a combination of guttural attack and mocking attitude. Later on, in postproduction, Wes and his sound mixers slowed down the voice track a tad, which gave Freddy's voice more bass and resonance. We were among the first films to control the pitch of a character's voice using some hardware called Varispeed, but they couldn't quite nail the process down, and at times the sound guys dialed it down too low and Freddy sounded distorted and lethargic, like an android that was running out of juice. However, some believe that the extra scootch of slow-down added to the creepiness factor and worked in our favor. (In later *Nightmare* movies, I spoke even deeper and a bit faster during the takes, so after the editors worked their magic, the pitch and cadence would sound more natural. Such as, if I said, "Welcometoprimetimebitch" at warp speed in front of the camera, it could come out sounding like "Welcome . . . to . . . prime . . . time . . . bitch . . ." after the final mix. There was a lot of trial and error, but we eventually solved it.)

And then, the shoot.

In one of those weird juxtapositions that makes Hollywood such a wonderful place to work, *A Nightmare on Elm Street* was shot at the old Desilu Studios, the very same Desilu Studios named for Desi Arnaz and Lucille Ball, the very same Desilu Studios that was home to *I Love Lucy* and *The Dick Van Dyke Show*. The irony of our horror flick being housed under the very same roof where television's classic comedy sitcoms originated wasn't lost on any of us. This same soundstage was also where *The Andy Griffith Show* was filmed. I shudder to think what Freddy would have done to little Opie.

Since most of the cast was young and inexperienced, I was only familiar with a few of the actors, but there was one person in particular I was looking forward to working with: John Saxon, who was playing the heroine Nancy's father, Lieutenant Don Thompson. John had been starring in movies since 1954 and had worked with Jimmy Stewart in *Mr. Hobbs Takes a Vacation*, and Robert Redford in *War Hunt* and *Electric Horseman*, and Bruce Lee in *Enter the Dragon*, and, most impressively to me, Marlon Brando in *The Appaloosa*. (One of my most prized possessions is my *Appaloosa* lobby card, which John autographed and hangs in a place of honor in my little Santa Fe adobe.)

Ronee Blakley, who played Nancy's mother, was no slouch either. She was nominated for an Oscar for her vulnerable performance in one of the seminal movies of the 1970s, Robert Altman's *Nashville*, and she'd dated the brilliant German director Wim Wenders, so, with one foot in the independent-film camp, and one in Euro-cinema, I thought she was the height of cool. She was flattered when, on one of the first days of shooting while we were sitting next to each other in makeup, I mentioned to her that soon after I wrapped *The Last of the Cowboys,* one of the actresses from that film and I trekked out to the venerable Palomino, a country-and-western bar deep in the Valley to hear her perform some of the songs from *Nashville.* I don't know how Ronee felt about having Freddy Krueger as a county-western fan; maybe she would've been more at home if I'd worn a cowboy hat instead of my fedora.

I was almost always the first actor at the studio because I had to endure the three-hour makeup application. On the third morning of the shoot, I was trying to get comfortable in one of the old Desilu makeup chairs, as David once again cold-glued the Freddy puzzle pieces to my mug, when in walked our star, our Nancy, the lovely Heather Langenkamp. Heather was twenty, and looked like a petite version of Brooke Shields. A bright, delightful girl and talented newcomer, her biggest role to date had been an appearance in Francis Ford Coppola's *The Outsiders;* unfortunately, her work had been left on the cutting-room floor.

A few minutes later, Johnny Depp strolled in. Johnny was a baby-faced twenty-one-year-old who, in the right light, could've passed for sixteen—which probably helped him land the lead in John Waters' *Cry-Baby* six years later. He was still three years away from becoming a TV star thanks to *21 Jump Street* and was clinging to his rockabilly roots. He'd had a band back in Florida, and with his slicked-back hair, long sideburns, pointy-toed boots, and fifties shirts he certainly looked as if he should be fronting a rock group. He was a bit shy and polite, and everybody on the set took to him instantly, especially the ladies.

So there I am getting glued and painted by David Miller, once again getting basted with that damn K-Y jelly so I'll appear nice and shiny under the lights, just like a pervert who'd been burned alive by a bunch of pissed-off vigilante parents.

I nodded hello to Heather and Johnny, then stared back at myself in the mirror. I was unrecognizable. I didn't see Robert Englund, a thirty-six-year-old veteran of a score of films and dozens of TV shows. All I saw was some guy whose face was buried under mounds of crap, parked between two of the most attractive young actors I'd ever seen, wondering if I'd made the right decision in taking this part. Here I was approaching forty, playing a monster who had barely any dialogue . . . and feeling completely envious of these kids. Heather and Johnny had their entire careers, their whole journey through Hollywood, ahead of them. And there I sat, cooking like a soft-boiled egg, and itching under that foam latex shit, while Heather and Johnny had little, personal electric fans keeping them cool and perspiration-free as they were gently powdered and pampered. As if they even needed any makeup.

I realized I could use this envy. No, *Freddy* could use it.

I could take my jealousy and resentment of their youth, beauty, and potential and give it to my character. During the more gruesome scenes and difficult special FX sequences, that envy would be the perfect Lee Strasberg sense-memory substitute to call upon. In my new interpretation, Freddy hated kids because they represent the future, something he'd never have. This could help me understand why Freddy was the way he was, why he was compelled to torture and murder children. I didn't need to feel sympathy with Freddy to play him, just a modicum of empathy. This realization unlocked a door for me to understand the character Fred Krueger. I had the key now. This was an approach I could sink my claws into.

In fact, both Heather and Johnny were consummate professionals, whose company I enjoyed, and vice versa. Despite the gap in our ages, Johnny and I hit it off, and once in a while he would confide in me. One night after we wrapped at the same time, we went out for a beer, and he shared a story about his rockabilly band. They weren't scoring many gigs, so Johnny decided to make a few exploratory trips out to California and give acting a try. He told me, "I knew it was time to move for good when I realized it was March and my Christmas tree was still up in my apartment." I flashed on an image of Johnny, with his Elvis hair, wearing a leather jacket, tight black jeans, and rockabilly boots, smoking a cigarette, staring sadly at a pile of brown pine needles on his apartment floor, sighing, "Time to move on. Yep. Time to move on."

IT BECAME SO MATTER-OF-FACT for everyone to see me in the Freddy makeup on the set every day that people started having a blasé attitude toward the character. They weren't scared of him, because it was my personality behind the mask between takes, and I'm not a scary guy. Still, I was committed to the role, but not to the degree that I'd run around the set slashing my fellow actors with my claw blades; I just wanted to keep them a little on edge, keep them wondering if maybe I was a bit wrong in the head. One thing I did to keep Heather off-balance was regale her with off-color jokes in the makeup room. I cadged fresh material each morning from the Teamsters over breakfast burritos. When I ran out of jokes, I playfully teased her until she either laughed or blushed or glared at me and said, "Knock it off, Robert, I mean it!" I wanted her to be at ease with me because we had several fight scenes and stunts together, and she needed to trust me and know that I'd zig when she zagged, and I'd zag when she zigged. If the trust wasn't there, she wouldn't be able to go all out, and the scene wouldn't work, so I was careful never to cross the line with Heather or make her feel uncomfortable. Over the years, however, I am sure I left enough thumbprint-size bruises on her that she probably qualified for extra stunt pay. I hope she'll forgive me.

As is the case on many movie sets, the catering on *Nightmare* sucked, so one sunny afternoon during meal break, Johnny Depp, Nick Corri, and I wandered over to the Thai restaurant across the street from the studio for a late lunch. We were seated in a booth in the back of the restaurant, and the kitchen had swinging double doors. I was facing the kitchen, so each time one of those doors opened, the fluorescent kitchen light spilled out onto our booth. Right after the server took our order, an elderly Asian waiter pushed backward through the doors from the kitchen, carrying a tray loaded with food and drinks. He turned in to the dining room, took one horrified look at my face illuminated in the harsh light, and stopped cold—oh, did I forget to mention I was still decked out in complete Freddy drag?—then the swinging door smacked him on the ass, and he dropped the tray. In a clatter of plates and glassware, a three-course lunch special hit the deck. He looked scared, ashamed, and then he scurried back into the kitchen.

He wasn't seen for the rest of our meal, and I felt terrible. I was genuinely concerned that I'd scared the old guy to death or maybe got the poor SOB fired. I thought it might be a good idea to limit Freddy to the soundstage from then on. But my resolve was weak, and Mr. Krueger would still be making unscheduled public appearances.

During one of our night shoots, I had a lot of time to kill, so, again in full Freddy regalia, I went on a little drive with a couple of friends who'd come to visit me on the set. Right after we turned onto Sunset Boulevard, we passed a couple of hookers. My pal who was driving gave the girls a once-over, then broke into a freaky smile.

He threw the car in reverse, backed up, opened his window, and motioned one of the girls over to the car. She teetered over in her stilettos; she had teased, distinctly 1980s big hair, a black leather miniskirt, and an acid-washed denim jacket with nothing on underneath. She seductively bent over and asked my friend, "Can I help you boys?"

He leered at her and said, "Yeah. We have a buddy here, and he served in 'Nam, and he got burned pretty bad there. We were wondering how much it would cost to, um, service him."

She said, "Where is he?"

My friend cocked his thumb at me in the backseat. "Right here."

When she leaned in the car to check me out, I let rip the biggest, ballsiest Freddy laugh I could muster, then lunged at the window.

The hooker screamed, ran down the block as fast as her five-inch heels would allow, tits bouncing, wig askew, stumbling back to her posse of pros.

I found ways to amuse myself on promotional tours as well. Once in Chicago, after a mob scene at an in-store signing session in the Midwest's oldest mom-and-pop video store, we escaped in a limo and found ourselves lost in an adjacent working-class neighborhood. We ran into a bunch of kids playing street hockey, and stopped to ask them for directions. After they cleared out of the street to let us through, I sprung up through the limo's sunroof—still in full makeup—and roared, *"You're all my children now!"* One of the kids yelled, "Yo, Freddy, you wanna get in on the game? We got some extra sticks." Not exactly the reaction I was shooting for.

Late one afternoon, after I'd finished shooting all my scenes, I tore off my makeup in a rush and headed to NBC in beautiful downtown Burbank for a *TV Guide* photo shoot to promote the television series *V,* which was going to commence shooting almost immediately after *Nightmare* wrapped. It had never been my dream to appear in *TV Guide,* but now that it was happening, I had to admit to myself that I was kind of excited.

As I sped through the winding canyon that links Hollywood to the Valley, I caught a glimpse of myself in the rearview mirror: my entire face was pink and swollen. I realized that in my haste, over David Miller's vociferous objections, I'd removed the Freddy prosthetics too roughly. When I posed that afternoon with the cast of the *V* series—which included a young actor named Jeff Yagher, whose brother I'd soon come to know very, very well—I looked like a test pilot for Clearasil sporting a *Welcome Back, Kotter* Juan Epstein Jew-fro. To this day, that ugly vintage *TV Guide* publicity photo haunts me at film festivals and sci-fi/horror/fantasy conventions around the world.

* * *

THE LAST WEEK OF shooting, we did a scene in which I drag Amanda Wyss, the sexy, blond actress who played Tina, across the ceiling of her bedroom, a sequence that ultimately became one of the most visceral from the entire *Nightmare* franchise. Tina's bedroom was constructed as a revolving set, and before Tina and Freddy did their dance of death, Wes did a few POV shots of Nick Corri (aka Rod) staring at the ceiling in disbelief, then we flipped the room, and the floor became the ceiling and the ceiling became the floor, and Amanda and I went to work.

As was almost always the case when Freddy was chasing after a nubile young girl possessed by her nightmare, Amanda was clad only in her baby-doll nightie. Wes had a creative camera angle planned that he wanted to try, a POV shot from between Amanda's legs. Amanda, however, wasn't in the cameramen's union and wouldn't legally be allowed to operate the camera for the shot. Fortunately, Amy Haitkin, our director of photography's wife, was our film's focus puller and a gifted camera operator in her own right. Being a good sport, she peeled off her jeans and volunteered to stand in for Amanda. The makeup crew dabbed some fake blood onto her thighs, she lay down on the ground, Jacques handed her the camera, I grabbed her ankles, and Wes called, "Action."

After I dragged Amy across the floor/ceiling, I spontaneously blew her a kiss with my blood-covered claw; the fake blood on my blades was viscous, so that when I blew her my kiss of death, the blood webbed between my blades formed a bubble, a happy cinematic accident. The image of her pale, slender, blood-covered legs, Freddy looming over her, straddling the supine adolescent girl, knife fingers dripping, was surreal, erotic, and made for one of the most sexually charged shots of the movie. Unfortunately it got left on the cutting-room floor. If Wes had left it in, the MPAA—who always seemed to have it out for Mr. Craven—would definitely have tagged us with an X rating. You win some, you lose some.

Subscribing to the Roger Corman school of getting the most bang for your buck, the revolving room was to be redressed and reused for Johnny Depp's death scene, the scene in which the Artist Soon to Be Known as Edward Scissorhands is swallowed, then regurgitated by his bed, accompanied by plenty of blood and guts. To get the effect right, the room had to slowly revolve so that gravity would cause the FX blood and guts to explode from Johnny's bed. To capture the sequence on film, Wes and Jacques had to be strapped into bucket seats that had been welded to the ceiling so that they and the camera would remain in a fixed position while the room rotated. I wasn't in the scene, but it was going to be one of the cooler moments of the shoot from a technical standpoint, so I hung out. This was can't-miss stuff.

I was standing off to the side backstage, barefoot, wearing a wifebeater T-shirt, jeans, with about half of my Freddy makeup removed; right next to me stood Heather, in those cute little pajamas she had on for most of the shoot. Wes called action, and the effects team spun the house clockwise. Unfortunately, they were supposed to have turned it counterclockwise, so a torrent of fake blood poured from the bed and began to fill the revolving room. The blood flood then overflowed through the door and windows of the set and all over the soundstage. Wes and Jacques got covered with the stuff, and we were afraid they might drown. But the more immediate problem was that like every film soundstage, the entire floor was littered with all kinds of electrical wiring and power boxes, which started hissing and sparking. Heather and I stared at the bloodbath, looked at each other, and then, like the big pussies that we were, hightailed it off the set, toward the exit. It was every monster for himself. I just hoped I wouldn't step on a nail and wind up with tetanus.

Freddy's climactic scene, when Nancy torches the monster, was the first fire stunt I'd ever been involved in. My stunt double, Tony Cecere—who, earlier that year, played the Stay Puft Marshmallow Man in *Ghostbusters*—was going to do all the fire work, but I had to be on the set for close-ups of me before and after Freddy got burned. It was to be one of the lengthiest interior fire stunts ever attempted, and I learned pretty quickly that even if the effects team is prepared to the max, indoor fire gags can be problematic. Any high school student who shows up for science class can tell you that fire eats up oxygen. So if you don't open up the stage door to let in oxygen while shooting a fire, stuntpeople can get a little loopy. And believe me, you don't want to be hanging out with a loopy stuntperson.

Everybody on the project worked around the clock and was happy to do so because we all believed in Wes, and our movie. Even near the end of the shoot, when we found out that New Line was running out of money and we might have trouble completing the film, we stuck with it, despite the pressure from the studio to hurry the fuck up, and the possibility of a bounced paycheck. To finish the movie, New Line had to sacrifice and sell off *Nightmare*'s potentially lucrative video rights, an expensive decision about which I'm certain they're eternally bittersweet.

In the end, Bob Shaye might have been the only studio boss who could've brought the *Nightmare* franchise to fruition. When I first met him, I thought, *This is a producer I can relate to.* He was young, good-looking, long-haired, and charismatic, far from your typical suit. I don't know what went on behind closed doors, but my dealings with him were genial and professional, and when we nearly ran out of money, I was practically the last person on the set to find out about our budget problems because I think Bob was trying to protect me.

Eventually, we got *Nightmare* in the can. After some good ol' R&R, it was back to *V* for me. Now that I was a pop-culture phenomenon, I decided to embrace it; so much for the classically trained Anglophile.

THERE MIGHT NOT HAVE been any Oscars in my future, but that didn't mean there wouldn't be other awards. The Italian TV guide magazine called *Telegatto*—which, loosely translated, means "television cat"—nominated me for Best Supporting Actor in a Miniseries for Willie in *V*. They flew me out to Milan first-class and expected the nominees and their dates to dress black tie for the award show. My girlfriend, Roxanne, forgot to pack anything formal for the event, so our hosts whisked her off to the Armani flagship store in the shadow of Milan's *duomo*, where she was given a beautiful navy blue silk dress. Me, I'd packed a rented tux, so I was good to go.

When we arrived in the piazza adjacent to La Scala opera house for the event, our limo was instantly surrounded by rabid Italian fans. I was pulled from the car, separated from Rox, and lifted above the crowd. Like a rock star in some giant mosh pit, I crowd-surfed to the entrance of the venue, where that evening I would beat out Richard Chamberlain for my first acting award ever. The cherry on the gelato would come later that night when Roxanne and I were seated between Catherine Deneuve and *The French Connection's* Fernando Rey for the postawards reception dinner. Pretty good company for a supporting alien. And if I ever find the Italian voice actor who dubbed my dialogue on *V,* I'll give him joint custody of my *Telegatto* award.

WHAT WITH ALL THE domestic and international success, NBC wisely offered Ken Johnson a weekly series, and Ken accepted. The network committed to twenty-two shows, and since my character Willie had attracted so much attention in the miniseries, my role was bulked up for the weekly show. While shooting an early episode, I was doing a stunt sequence with my costar Michael Ironside. We were driving in a van with the side door open, and in the scene we were supposed to haul a stuntman dressed as one of the storm-trooper aliens into the van, slam the door shut, and peel away. Sounds simple. And it was.

On the first take, I nailed it. Second take, nailed it again. Third take, ditto. On the fourth take, *Ooooooooh shit.*

I don't know why we needed to do it a fourth time because the first three felt perfect. But we were pros, and if Ken

Johnson's people wanted a fourth take, then Ken Johnson's people would get a fourth take, and we wouldn't complain. And that take was a problem from the get-go. Maybe the stunt driver was a little burned-out, because he pulled in noticeably faster and with a little more gusto than he had in the earlier takes, then he braked and we all slid across the van floor and crashed into the back of the front seat. Michael and the stunt-man hung on to the front seat, but I couldn't get a grip, and when the stunt driver shifted into gear and floored it, the van lurched forward and I slid back toward the rear of the van. My head hit the unlocked back door, making contact with the door handle at a perfect angle—the perfect angle, that is, if I were trying to open the door with my face. The doors flew open, and I crashed onto the street.

Surprisingly, I was more or less okay, aside from a huge gash on my forehead. Michael stared at my face, pointed at the nasty scar on his cheek, and said, "You see this? I got this up in Canada. They took me to some Eskimo hack who sewed me up with a whalebone or something. Let's not mess around here. If you don't get this fixed *now*, and get this fixed *right*, you're going to have a big scar forever right on that forehead of yours. We're getting you to a plastic surgeon *immediately*." (Michael was absolutely right. Plastic surgeons stitch you up differently from the doctors at the emergency room so that you heal with minimal scarring. This is excellent advice for anybody who doesn't want a permanent scar on their precious kid's face.)

We'd been filming in the foothills near the Santa Anita Race Track, in San Marino, just east of Pasadena, right by where the original version of *Invasion of the Body Snatchers* was shot. Fortunately, it was an upscale area, and upscale areas in

Los Angeles tend to be filled with plastic surgeons, so within minutes after the accident, thanks to Michael, I was sitting in the waiting room of a famous plastic surgeon, about to get my gash repaired. Once I learned that this doctor was the same plastic surgeon who had worked on Michael Jackson after his hair caught on fire during the filming of that Pepsi commercial, I knew I was in good hands. If he fixed the King of Pop, he could fix Willie the alien lizard, no problem.

The doctor took us into his office and explained the procedure, which sounded fine to me. He then pulled out a bottle of Scotch, poured me two fingers, gave me a local anesthetic, and went about the business of making me beautiful again.

The surgery took place on Friday evening. By Sunday morning, my forehead was so black-and-blue and ballooned up that I thought I'd never get offered a role for the rest of my life. I looked like Quasimodo in the *Hunchback of Notre Dame*. I had a meltdown and yelled at Roxanne, *"I'll never act again! I'll have to become a director. Or, God forbid, a writer!"* I was whining like a big baby. But as the week progressed, the swelling gradually went down. The surgeon had given me some vitamin E, and a couple of my hippie friends had given me some aloe vera plants to rub on the wound, and by the following Sunday, it was mostly gone. Thirty-seven stitches, and only the faintest trace of a scar. (So now the misshapen nose that both Kris Kristofferson and Richard Gere had contributed to was accompanied by that faint thread of a scar over my left eyebrow. I was beginning to look like a punch-drunk welterweight.) Thanks, Doc, thank you vitamin E oil, thank you aloe vera juice, and thank you, thank you, thank you, Michael Ironside.

A week later, the phone rang: "Is this Mr. Englund?"

"Yeah."

"The Robert Englund who was injured on the set of *V?*"

"Um, who is this?"

"Don't worry about who this is. The only thing you should worry about is suing Warner Bros."

"Why would I sue Warner Bros.?"

"Negligence. You shouldn't have been anywhere near that van. You're not a stuntman. You're an actor. Warners didn't look out for you. They don't look out for any of their actors. I'll help you put together a case. You initiate a suit, and I'll cut you a check for a million dollars."

"Who is this?"

"Don't worry about who this is. You in or not?"

"Not." I'd developed a great working relationship with Warner Bros. over the years, and I had no interest in suing them, especially since my injury had all but disappeared. I slammed down the phone.

The next week, he called again, and I didn't let him get three sentences into his pitch before I hung up. I never heard from him again, but I have a suspicion of who he was. The scandal and litigation over the *Twilight Zone: The Movie* tragedy—in which actor Vic Morrow and two children were killed—still permeated the industry. I think some ambulance chasers were trying to get me to be part of a class-action suit against Warners. Hollywood had always been good to me, so it didn't occur to me to sue; besides, I didn't want to bite the hand that was feeding me.

* * *

THE STAR OF *V*, Faye Grant, was one of the most savvy TV actresses I've worked with, something that some of the actors would get a little frustrated with. For example, in a scene, Faye would occasionally avoid eye contact, sometimes turning her back to the camera and busying herself with props. It was almost as if she were trying to hide from the prying lens. I didn't know what the hell she was up to and didn't bother asking, because I figured it was her business and she probably wouldn't want to discuss it.

I was just as confused as the other cast members, until I started paying close attention to her performance when I watched our show every Friday night at home. I realized that Faye was cherry-picking "moments." She wished to highlight certain lines of dialogue, but instead of emphasizing those lines, she would underplay or throw away her other dialogue. Then when she had a moment she wanted to pop, she would look up for the camera, and letting her light hit her face and her eyes *just right*, she would literally own the moment. Faye was so in control of what she was doing that when it came time for the editors to piece together the show, they had no choice but to use the takes and angles that she'd silently dictated. It wasn't about a lack of generosity; it was about protecting her work and making it rise above standard television acting. This wasn't the kind of thing that was taught at ADA, or anywhere else for that matter. Faye's TV technique helped me understand that I still had plenty to learn.

A couple of years later, I saw Faye performing on Broadway in an excellent production of *Singing in the Rain*, which was directed by the great choreographer Twyla Tharp. Faye played the silent-screen star whose shrill, irritating voice would prevent her from making the transition to talkies. She was a completely different physical presence onstage than the actress I had worked with on TV. Her comedy work was deft, and her vocal transformation astounding—truly a versatile turn.

After the show, I went backstage and waited in the hall by her dressing room, right next to Andy Warhol and Leonard Bernstein. When Faye finally came out, I gave her a big hug and told her how impressed I was. Then I confided in her: "I learned so much about film acting from watching you work on *V.*" (Faye hasn't stopped doing great work. In 2002, she again exhibited her versatility when she essayed a flamboyant Auntie Mame–type character, Tattie McKee, on the underrated cable series *State of Grace.*)

THE WEEK BEFORE *A Nightmare on Elm Street* was released nationwide, I was invited to my first science-fiction convention; this one was held in New York City at the old Roosevelt Hotel on Madison and Forty-fifth, near the Diamond District. At that time, *Nightmare* barely registered on my radar; the *V* series was such a success that it was taking up all of my time and energy.

The convention organizers—who had paid me a generous fee to appear—set up a table in the lobby, where I could sign autographs, memorabilia, and shoot the shit with the fans. The line of people who wanted to chat with Willie snaked through the lobby, went out the door, and around the block. It was a miserably rainy day, but that hadn't stopped the diehards, who'd waited in line since dawn to spend a couple of minutes with me. I'd known *V* was big, but seeing such a sizable crowd turn out in the Big Apple *really* brought it home for me. The first hour, fans politely gave me *V*-oriented merchandise to sign, asked a question or two, and went on their merry way. But then things got a little strange and the line began to evolve.

My fans were no longer wearing homemade *V* costumes or sci-fi nerd gear. They had on Ramones T-shirts, ripped jeans, spiked collars around their necks, with multiple facial piercings. There were girls with magenta hair, and guys with eight-inch-high Mohawks. They were rock 'n' roll. They were heavy metal. They were punk.

And they all loved Freddy Krueger.

In the midst of all this, who wanders over but Bob Shaye from New Line, who was there to take me out for a late lunch. Bob took one look at the long line, and a huge smile broke out on his face. "Shit, the movie hasn't even opened wide."

"Yeah, Bob, it's great." Then, politely, I added, "But I have to tell you that most of the fans are here because of *V*."

He either didn't hear me or chose to ignore it. "Yep. *Nightmare*'s a hit."

"I think they're here for *V*, Bob."

"Nah. *Nightmare*."

I glanced across the lobby and out into the rain, and sure enough, Bob was right. An army clad in wet black leather was huddled under awnings and stretching down the street waiting to meet Freddy.

I was pleased about my expanding fan base from the punk/

heavy-metal contingent, but my mind was still in *V*-land. The TV series was a bona fide smash, and I was making good money. I didn't earn much on *Nightmare*, and in terms of box office, it could still go either way. New York City was the punk/heavy-metal capital of the world, but how would Freddy play in Peoria? And what about those secondary markets such as Miami and Dallas, where there weren't as many movie theaters? Did people still care about horror movies there? I knew *Nightmare* was a good little flick, but I couldn't share Bob's over-the-top optimism, not because I didn't believe in the movie, but rather because I'd never been part of a major horror project and couldn't venture a guess as to how the genre's fans would react.

The next week, I went to see everybody's favorite comic magic team, Penn and Teller, perform off-Broadway, and in the middle of the second act they cracked a Freddy Krueger joke. (I don't know if they knew I was out in the audience, but even if they did, how could they recognize me without the claw?) It was another sign that *A Nightmare on Elm Street* was beginning to enter the zeitgeist. Something was brewing, and it wasn't just in Freddy's boiler room.

What had begun as Wes Craven's frightening memory of a childhood encounter with a menacing man and cost a piddling $1.8 million to make, ended up grossing a whopping $26.5 million in domestic box office and launched a horror empire. Wes had created a monster. He was my Dr. Frankenstein, and I liked it. I thought, *Hey, I just might stick with this scary shit for a while.*

CHAPTER
6

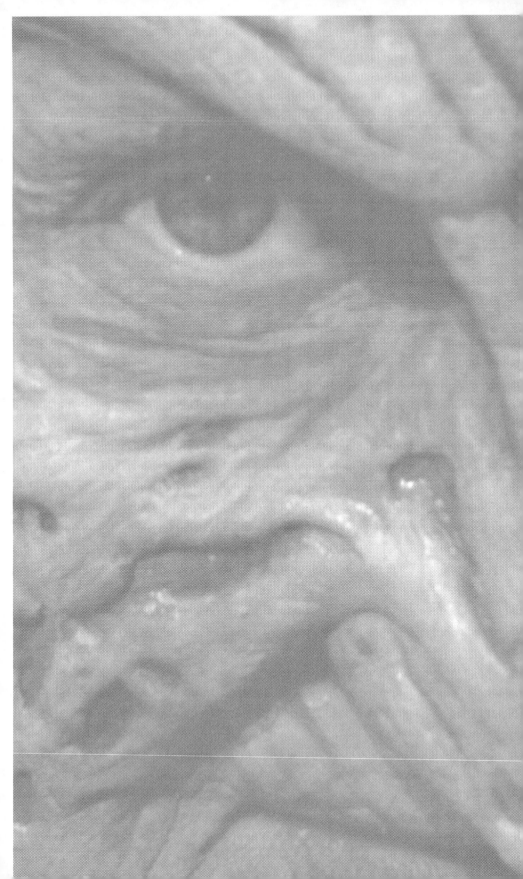

NIGHTMARE #6:

While catnapping in the hour before dawn during the filming of the original *A Nightmare on Elm Street*, I was awakened by rapping on my trailer door. The second assistant director was calling for me on set. I sat up disoriented, in the half-light of the dimmed makeup mirror bulbs. I caught a glimpse of movement in the shadowed depths of the mirror. Groggy from sleep, distracted by my morning-mouth breath, I was shocked to see a disfigured, bald man staring back at me. My heart skipped a beat or five, and then I realized it was just Freddy staring back at me. I'd forgotten I was still in makeup. The knocking resumed and I recovered from my momentary fright. However, that image of Freddy deep in the shadows, mimicking my movements in the mirror like some Marx Brothers bit from hell has stayed with me to this day.

*I*N THE MID-EIGHTIES, EVEN IF YOUR MOVIE was a hit, a sequel wasn't guaranteed—the *Star Wars* and *Raiders of the Lost Ark* franchises notwithstanding. Today, films go into production with a blueprint for as many as five follow-ups—probably sequel scripts for fifteen Batman flicks are sitting on some producer's shelf—but back then, it was one at a time, and if you were offered the opportunity for a "part two," you were grateful.

They offered me a *Nightmare* "part two." I was grateful.

I hadn't made much money on the first one—the biggest chunk of our "budget" (yes, those quotation marks denote sarcasm) went toward makeup and effects—and it soon became clear during my contract negotiations that I wasn't going to get rich on *Freddy's Revenge* either. But I'd had a great time on the first movie, which had garnered quite the cult audience, plus the shoot was in the summer, during my hiatus for *V*, so I signed on the dotted line and prepared myself once again to commit murder and mayhem. When New Line sent me the script, I couldn't have been happier with my decision, because the story felt *right*.

But something about the interesting plot bothered me: one of the major rules that Wes had established on *A Nightmare on Elm Street* had been broken—Freddy was taken out of the dreams. In *Nightmare 2*, Freddy would be allowed to manifest outside of the dreamscape. It didn't hurt the quality of the script, but it messed up the continuity. On the plus side, I thought the bisexual-slash-homoerotic subtext was edgy and contemporary, and I appreciated how the plot investigated both the social-class system and the rise of suburban malaise. This may sound pretentious and overanalytical, but I believe that Freddy represented what looked to be a bad future for the postboomer generation. It's possible that Wes believed the youth of America were about to fall into a pile of shit—virtually all the parents in the *Nightmare* movies were flawed, so how could these kids turn out safe and sane?—and he might have created Freddy to represent a less-than-bright future.

I was the only major cast member from *A Nightmare on Elm Street* to return for the sequel, *A Nightmare on Elm Street 2: Freddy's Revenge,* but Johnny, Heather, et al. weren't the only missing faces. David Miller, my beloved makeup man, was busy with *The Terminator, Cocoon,* and the fifth installment of the *Friday the 13ᵗʰ* series. He was replaced by Kevin Yagher, brother of Jeff Yagher, one of my costars from *V. Nightmare 2* was only Kevin's third movie, but he was so talented that in time he became one of the heavyweights of the industry. In 1988, he created Chucky for the *Child's Play* film franchise, then, eleven years later, in a six-degrees-of-Kevin-Bacon kind of coincidence, Kevin wrote and coproduced the Johnny Depp flick *Sleepy Hollow.*

Kevin and I were instant friends. Creatively speaking, he had a different style from David Miller, whose makeup was slightly thicker and more dramatic. With David, if the camera was farther away and the light was just right, Freddy's features were easier to delineate. With Kevin, the closer the camera got, the better it looked. I liked them both, and I never found out why David was replaced. Maybe it was about money. Maybe everybody had got ulcers worrying about how the makeup would look on the first one. Or maybe they just wanted some new blood, if you will. Kevin also managed to make the facial makeup practically prophylactic, which enabled me to be more expressive—the audience would be able to see even the slightest twitch of my eye, or a tiny sneer.

Kevin was one of the funnier guys I've ever worked with. During the hours and hours we spent together perfecting the new Freddy face, he'd do nonstop, dead-on impressions, my favorite of which were his dialogues between Dean Martin and Jerry Lewis, commenting on his progress with the makeup, scolding himself in Dean's voice if he made a mistake, and praising himself as Jerry when he liked how something looked. It was like having my own personal stand-up comedy team, and believe me, I needed it. But the most noticeable change on *Freddy's Revenge* was in the director's chair, with Jack Sholder replacing Wes Craven. One of the first foodies I'd ever met, Jack and I became fast friends. *Nightmare 2* was only his second feature, the first being 1982's *Alone in the Dark*, another horror flick for New Line starring Donald Pleasence, Martin Landau, and Jack Palance, and cowritten by one Bob Shaye. Jack knew the horror world, he knew how to relate to his actors, he was a crack editor, and he knew where to find the best dim sum in Los Angeles. Freddy was in good hands.

No future Johnny Depp was in our cast, but that didn't mean we didn't have some promising kids. Kim Myers, who played Lisa, was a wonderful young actress who was making her film debut, and when I met her, the first thing that popped into my head was, *Jeez, this girl bears an uncanny resemblance to Meryl Streep.* Meryl wasn't quite an icon yet, but she was getting there, and I thought that having Freddy torment a teenage version of *The French Lieutenant's Woman* was pretty cool. And Bob Shaye, Mr. New Line himself, played a bartender at an S&M club. I'm not sure what that says about Bob, but there you have it.

This second time around, I had a better idea of what to expect on the shoot, but I was still a little nervous about the two-part fire stunt during the pool-party scene. Naturally, my stuntman would actually be dealing with the flames, but as talented as our effects team was, fire could be unpredictable.

Turned out, so could stuntmen.

My stuntman scored a bit part as one of the jocks at the party, and he had a couple lines, which pleased me because that meant he'd get a bump in pay, as well as qualify for his Screen Actors Guild card. When it came time to film the first part of the fire stunt, the guy was still on the set, finishing up his scene, so our fire wrangler asked if I could do a quick fire walk. "It's simple," he said. "All you have to do is go through that arbor gate over there as it spontaneously combusts from your evil energy. And you gotta do that sexy Freddy walk. You know what I mean?"

"I know what you mean."

"The one thing is, you have to walk real slow. You can't rush it. You can't be nervous about it. You're Freddy Fucking Krueger, and Freddy Fucking Krueger isn't bothered by some pussy little fire."

I said, "Yeah, but Robert Fucking Englund is."

"Don't worry. You'll have water gel on your hat, and we'll all be standing by with our fire extinguishers." He then smiled. "We're hoping to do a *Nightmare 3*, so we don't want you to get all burned up."

"Very funny."

We did two passes. The first one was hot. The second one was hotter. But I survived. My sweater was smoldering, but no fire extinguishers were necessary.

I shot a couple more scenes that night, but we had to wrap before we could get much else done, because we were in Pasadena, and the Pasadena city council had decreed that any movie filming there had to shut down by 10 p.m. So as usual, because of the slow makeup removal, Kevin and I were still on the set long after everybody else left. We were drinking some beer, shooting the shit, taking our sweet old time.

When we got to the section of Freddy skin around my temple and ear, Kevin stopped. "Um, Robert?"

"Yeah?"

"We have a problem." He didn't say it in a Jerry Lewis voice, so I suspected he was serious.

"What kind of problem?"

"The kind of problem where some of this shit is stuck."

Turns out that my slow walk through the fire had caused a part of the foam latex prosthetics to bond to a portion of my forehead. We spent the next five hours meticulously taking off that fused latex piece by tiny piece. Kevin only removed one of my sideburns and a small chunk of my eyebrow that night, which we considered a victory.

* * *

FOR THE FILM'S CLIMACTIC scene, we were shooting at a 1930s-era power station, an atmospheric interior that translated perfectly onto film. I was up on a perforated catwalk, portraying Freddy on his last legs. I was in the corner, down for the count, and about to get burned alive again; the scene was to be completed with an animatronic version of Freddy's head and torso being immolated. Kevin had created the puppet, and it was an uncanny look-alike, so much so that over the years I've autographed hundreds of photos of that fucking dummy.

The effects crew covered my arm and sweater with more of that water gel, so I could stick my arm in the fire before turning it over to the robot for the face-melting sequence. One of the guys said, "Okay, Robert, here's the deal. Step one, stick your hand in the fire. Step two, count to five. Step three, get the fuck out of there. Got it?"

"Hand in fire, count to five, get the fuck out. Got it. Now let's light this candle!"

The fire was lit, Jack called action, and I watched the flames inch closer and closer to me on the catwalk railing. The fire reached my hand and I marveled at how the water gel had protected me. Sure, it was a little toasty, but there was no pain, no burning, no acrid smell of seared flesh. I watched the flickering flames. I imagined how cool I must look.

Thing is, I forgot step two. I was so hypnotized by the flames that I neglected to count.

Fortunately, I survived in one piece, but Jack wanted to try another couple of takes, so I might still get fried before the day was out. We did another take, and I forgot to count again. One of the effects guys yelled, "Jesus Christ, Robert, you're still waiting too long to take your arm out! Count to five!"

Feeling a little woozy, I said, "Five. Right. Great."

I quickly shook my head to clear out some cobwebs. Then I remembered one of the key lessons I'd learned on *A Nightmare on Elm Street*: fire eats oxygen, and without oxygen people get goofy. That ended my desire to do any more fire stunts. From that moment on, I'd leave it to the professionals. I'd grown to love Freddy, but I wasn't ready to die for him.

I suspect that Bob Shaye, Wes Craven, et al. weren't ready to sacrifice me for the sake of a stunt, either—especially after they got the final numbers. *Nightmare 2*, which cost $3 million to make, hauled in over $30 million domestically. Which begged the question, would there be a number three?

CHAPTER 7

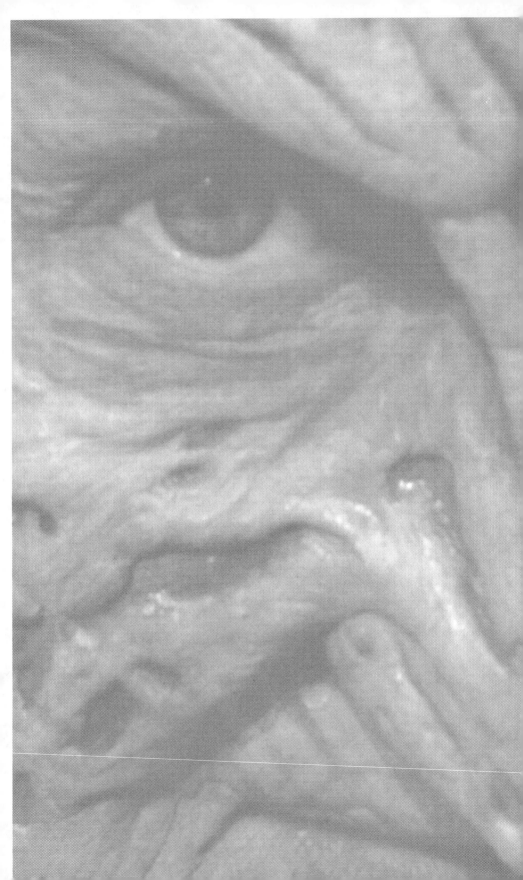

NIGHTMARE #7:

There's a hall. A hall of doors. But I never seem to go through the doors. As I get closer to a door, it recedes in perspective like the dolly zoom camera effect Spielberg used on Roy Scheider when he first sees the shark in *Jaws*. It literally gives me an upset stomach. This image frequently bookends a dream of mine that is about to go bad. It's a warning. It telegraphs an impending nightmare.

S OON AFTER I FINISHED UP WITH *NIGHTMARE 2*, *V* was canceled. The show was one of those unfortunate casualties of bad network-television decisions. Apparently the profit-and-loss statements at the end of the first season of this big-budget show weren't looking good to NBC. It was popular, and I think the choice to cancel it was premature. Too bad. *V* had been an important chapter in my career and a cherished experience for me, but it was time to move on.

Thankfully I managed to keep busy—that's what us utility actors strive to do, keep working—with a few TV movies (e.g., *Infidelity* with Kirstie Alley and Courtney Thorne-Smith) and another network series (*Downtown* with Mariska Hargitay and Blair Underwood). It was good to be working, especially alongside the beautiful young Mariska, but without *V*, playing Freddy again seemed more appealing than ever—especially since without regular, highly visible film and TV roles, I might wind up on the cutting-room floor, or backsliding into parts like Biker #2 on *Nancy Drew* or a recurring stoolie on *Police Story, Police Woman,* or, God forbid, *Police Dog.*

Fortunately, *Nightmare* finally started raking in *serious* bucks for New Line, not only as a result of its U.S. success, but also because Freddy was getting much love internationally. This was a welcome perk because the only overseas love I'd ever received was the little award I'd been given for *V* in Italy, and the room-service hooker I'd been assigned in the Philippines. The worldwide success of the first two installments meant that New Line was more than happy to green-light *A Nightmare on Elm Street 3: Dream Warriors*. Which meant that for the time being, I wouldn't be returning to play Thug #1 on *Manimal*.

To me, the screenplay for *Dream Warriors* was the best *Nightmare* script to date, probably because it was written by a trio of Hollywood heavies: Wes Craven, Frank Darabont, and Bruce Wagner. Since the first *Nightmare*, Wes's most notable, memorable work was in CBS's updated version of *The Twilight Zone*, which proved that he still had as good of a grasp on the surreal and scary as anybody in the industry. Darabont was a Hollywood newcomer, but anybody who read the script could tell that the guy had some serious chops, and probably wouldn't be surprised that he'd later turn the Stephen King novella *Rita Hayworth and Shawshank Redemption* into one of the great films of the nineties. Bruce Wagner was also a talented newbie who would make a mark several years later with his Hollywood-based novels *Force Majeure* and *I'm Losing You*. Together, these writers concocted a clever little sequel that I think deserves consideration as one of the hundred greatest horror films of all time. Over the last twenty-five years, I've met tens of thousands of Freddy fans, and I think it is fair to say that if they were all polled, *Nightmare 3* would win as fan favorite.

Chuck Russell, who also had a hand in the screenplay, was making his directorial debut, but as was the case with Jack Sholder from *Nightmare 2*, the guy overcame his lack of experience with sheer moxie and artistry. This was by far the most complex of the *Nightmare* movies to date—bigger sets, bigger effects, bigger cast—but Chuck handled the whole production like a wily veteran. (Seven years later, he directed the seminal Jim Carrey FX vehicle *The Mask*, whose $18 million budget was only slightly eclipsed by the combined total of the first four *Nightmare* flicks. He would also go on to helm *The Scorpion King* in 2002.)

Chuck came across as the hardest-working director in showbiz, always the first to arrive on the set, and always the last to leave, possibly because he was enjoying the opportunity to play with that big toy-train set that a Hollywood movie can be. The late eighties was one of the most exciting times in Hollywood for anybody with an affinity for special effects . . . that is, if you had a big budget. *Nightmare 3*'s budget was $5 million, which was barely enough to cover an explosion on *Indiana Jones and the Temple of Doom*. But luckily for us, Chuck and New Line assembled a crew who had the heart, skills, and vision to make our effects *appear* expensive. Chuck would ask, "Guys, I need Freddy to burn like the Nazis in *Raiders of the Lost Ark*. Can you do it for a hundred bucks?" and our guys would say, "Shit, Chuck, we can name that tune for $99.99." This gifted young FX crew could watch a new effect in a big-budget movie and duplicate it for pennies on the dollar.

Bob Shaye and his creative gang at New Line also assembled one hell of a cast for the movie. Heather Langenkamp was back and, as always, a real trouper. The character Kristen was played by a nineteen-year-old knockout named Patricia Arquette, whom all the young males in the cast desired. These lovelorn boys were writing her mash notes and buying her flowers, and one particularly desperate young man turned to me for advice. He whined to me, "Patricia's sooooo beautiful. I'm never gonna feel love like this ever again. What should I do?" He even asked me to help him with a love letter. I felt like Cyrano de Goddamn Bergerac.

A pre-*Matrix* Laurence Fishburne had a small part, and Dick Cavett and Zsa Zsa Gabor appeared in cameos. With Zsa Zsa in the movie, the already blurred lines between on-screen dreams and reality became even more surreal. Ms. Gabor, who was probably just grateful to be asked to appear in a movie again, apparently didn't read the script or bother to do any research on the *Nightmare* flicks. I guess her agent told her, "I have a job for you," and all she said was "Great. Vhat time zhould I zhow up, dahlink?" not realizing that she was about to throw down with a burnt-to-a-crisp serial killer. During the fake talk show where she's interviewed by Dick Cavett, all her reactions seen on film were 100 percent genuine. She didn't know who the fuck Freddy was, so when I jumped out, she had a mild freak-out. Cavett, who always had his finger on the pulse of pop culture, knew exactly who and what he was dealing with and looked wholly unfazed and handled the whole faux TV interview with aplomb.

Also making her film debut, breathtaking young model/ actress Jennifer Rubin played Taryn, the spiky-haired, dream-warrior junkie-girl who gets a fatal heroin injection from Freddy. At one point, the track marks on Taryn's arms come to life and turn into little, hungry, sucking mouths. Those tiny mouths required an *extensive* special effects makeup session, with Jennifer having to hold her arm motionless for almost seven hours. The FX team did meticulous work, except for the minor error of putting the mouths on the wrong arm. *Major bummer.* Which, of course, meant Jennifer had to repeat the entire process.

The next morning, still half-asleep, I stumbled into the makeup FX room and was shocked to see the mirror covered with graffiti. The mystery tagger had used red lipstick instead of spray paint. Amid the lightning bolts, squiggles, and frowny faces, right in the middle was a single phrase: DA MAKEUP DONE GOT ME!!! Apparently, after almost a dozen hours in makeup, Jennifer snapped. I can't say I blame her one bit. There have been days in the makeup chair when I've contemplated arson.

I've heard stories about actors who have been in the business far longer than Jennifer who have had major issues with makeup too. In 1984, my old pal Gary Busey played football coach Bear Bryant in a biopic called *The Bear*, and apparently the age makeup made him itchy and self-conscious, and it drove him nuts. Lori Singer, the cello-playing beauty of *Fame* fame, reportedly suffered through and could barely endure an elaborate witch-makeup session in *Warlock*, courtesy of my old producer Roger Corman. In *The Bride*, Sting's contribution to the Frankenstein canon, the actor playing the creature apparently had such an intense allergic reaction to the makeup that production temporarily ground to a halt. And word on the street was that Leo DiCaprio despised the synthetic hair he had to wear as the aging Howard Hughes in *The Aviator*. Some people can handle it, some people can't. Getting that shit put on and taken off your face every day for hours on end can be a real bitch.

Some difficult moments also occurred outside the makeup room on the set of *Nightmare 3*. One evening, we were shooting a scene in Freddy's hellish boiler-room lair, using a converted warehouse across the street from the gritty, fortresslike Los Angeles County Jail. Heather and Patricia were supposed to run down the stairs from a high platform constructed near the warehouse's ceiling, wind their way through boiling cauldrons of multicolored *stuff*, and attack Freddy; this meant that the girls had to begin their entrance from a ledge where the actresses could barely stand up straight. Making matters worse, the night crew had just finished painting all the interior sets that morning, and some of the *stuff* bubbling away in the cauldrons was actually paint.

I was down below on the floor waiting for Chuck to call action, and I realized that the entire warehouse reeked—once all the stage lights had gone on, the still-wet scenery paint had heated up, and thanks in part to the solvents being released from the bubbling-paint effect, the fumes had gotten noxious. Down where I was, it smelled pretty bad, but I could live with it, so I didn't pay much attention to the odor. However, waiting for their cue up at the top of the set, Heather and Patricia almost succumbed to the poisoned air, especially Heather, who nearly passed out from the fumes and could have fallen God-knows-how-many feet to her death.

That night, after everybody went home, Kevin and I—whom people had started referring to as the Siamese Twins because we were practically glued together (literally, we spent so much time touching up the makeup with medical adhesive)—finished my makeup removal around four forty-five in the morning. With some Vaseline residue still on my face and a bit of crusty, dried fake blood coming out of my ear, we trudged out of the warehouse into the dawn, dragging ass

CIRCA SUMMER 1954 OR '55, Robbie "The Fish" Englund in the family pool.

SUMMER 1966, HOLLYWOOD: Starring in *The Rising of the Moon* by Lady Gregory, costarring Lindsay Doran (producer, *Sense and Sensibility*, *Stranger than Fiction*).

BEEBO CROZIER AND Elegant John: Taking a break between scenes with the great Henry Fonda on *Last of the Cowboys*, somewhere outside Palm Springs, 1976.

SPONGEBOB SHREDDING
IN the shadow of Bette
Davis's house, Laguna
Beach, 1998.

NANCY AND I enjoying
the sunset in Santa Fe,
New Mexico, on our
wedding day, October,
1988.

WILLIE IN THE paraffin wax and halved grape "frozen blisters" makeup in *V* with Jason Bernard, 1983. (*V* © WARNER BROS. INC. ALL RIGHTS RESERVED.)

LADY FROM SHANGHAI meets *Silence of the Lambs*: Taking a break with Ted Levine on the set of Stephen King's *The Mangler* in South Africa, 1994.

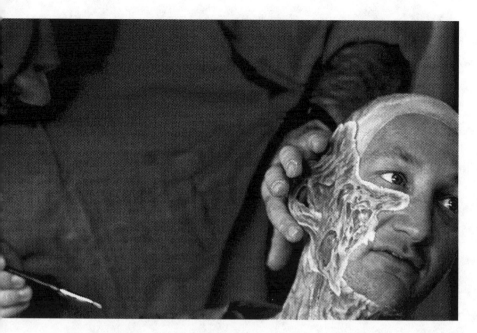

GETTING MY FREDDY makeup applied by Oscar winner and fellow mob survivor Howard Berger, 1988. (*A NIGHTMARE ON ELM STREET 4: THE DREAM MASTER* © THE FOURTH NEW LINE–HERON VENTURE. ALL RIGHTS RESERVED.)

IN THE SACK with Johnny Depp, 1984. (*A NIGHTMARE ON ELM STREET* © THE ELM STREET VENTURE. LICENSED BY: NEW LINE PRODUCTIONS. ALL RIGHTS RESERVED.)

HERE
GO aga
Nancy's sl
of the fi
makeup t
for *Freddy*
Jason, 20

NOT ANOTHER FIRE stunt?!?! With Ken Kerzinger in *Freddy vs. Jason,* 2003.

KIDDING AROUND ON the set of *Jamie Foxx*, 1999.

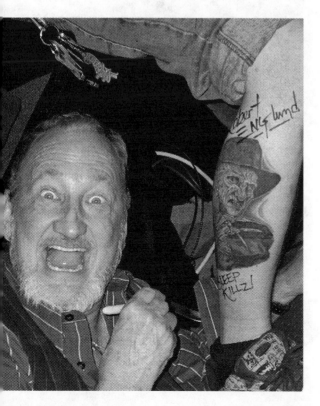

THIS GUY HAD my signature tattooed shortly after I signed his leg. Wish I had better handwriting! Check out RobertEnglund. com for a gallery of Freddy "tats." (PHOTO OF ROBERT WITH TOM ALBRIGHT COURTESY OF CORRINE ALBRIGHT.)

WATCHING VIDEO
REPLAY with the
Sicilian geniuses,
Cipri and Maresco,
2002.

THE DEVIL MADE
me do it! As Lucifer
making a Faustian
bargain with Al
Bundy (Ed O'Neill),
1997. (*MARRIED WITH
CHILDREN* COURTESY
SONY PICTURES
TELEVISION.)

because we were so fucking exhausted and starving. (I don't eat much when I have the Freddy makeup on because, when I do, the natural oils in food cause my lips to come unglued, and when my lips come unglued, Kevin comes running across the soundstage and attacks me with his little, stiff glue brush, and believe me, nobody needs that.) Parked fifty yards ahead of us, in the street in front of the jail, there was a hard-core Mexican catering truck, the kind that some people refer to as a roach coach or a ptomaine wagon. We were so hungry that we didn't care. If our burritos were seasoned with roaches, so be it.

Unless you've had a friend or relative serve any time, you probably don't know that in California, when you're released from jail, you're let out in the morning, bright and early, which was why a small crowd was in front of the security gate—mothers, daughters, sons, girlfriends, wives, all waiting for their loved ones to be sprung. Right behind all these friends and family members were about a dozen prostitutes. You might ask yourself, why would a bunch of hookers stand right in front of L.A. County Jail at the crack of dawn? Simple: the first thing some of these just-freed men want to do is to get laid. What these horny cons didn't realize (or did they?) was that a couple of the prostitutes were transgender, one of whom presumed that Kevin and I might be potential clients and cut in line to proposition us.

Kevin and I politely declined his/her invitation. But since I was still wearing almost as much makeup as the, ahem, young lady and was kind of sympathetic to her plight, I pulled out my wallet and said, "Let me treat you to some breakfast." The three of us stood there chowing down on the best burritos I'd ever tasted and watched the smoggy L.A. sun rise over the jail.

As the ex-cons trickled out of lockup and into the welcoming arms of family and friends, our new transgender acquaintance polished off her burrito, daintily dabbed her mouth with a napkin, touched up her lipstick, and declared, "Excuse me, gentlemen, but I have some dicks to suck." A little walk on the wild side. Cue Lou Reed.

AS WITH THE FIRST *Nightmare,* we shot a couple of interesting scenes that didn't make it into the final cut, most notably one featuring a female Freddy. One of the kids in the hospital has a Freddy dream in which he's being seduced by a sexy nurse. The nightmare evolves into a kinky S&M fantasy, but becomes less *M* and more *S* when the ropes that bind the kid to the bed become Freddy tongues, and the nurse's face morphs into Freddy's, but her topless torso, which features a pair of perfect *Playboy* breasts, remains smooth and inviting . . . that is, for a moment. All of a sudden, the veins in her areolas come to life and turn into Freddy-like burn scars and snake up her cleavage, past her neck, and onto her face. (I'm pretty sure Kevin enjoyed the four hours it took to apply makeup to those tits.) This troubling, erotic transformation didn't make the final cut for some reason. Occasionally I find myself signing bootleg stills from the missing sequence. Especially in Europe. Ooh la la!

After *Nightmare 3,* the Freddy Krueger phenomenon was in full swing: Freddy was making appearances in popular comic strips and in political cartoons on the editorial pages of daily newspapers. My old hero Johnny Carson started doing Krueger jokes, and references to Freddy appeared on TV and in major motion pictures, including one by none other than Tom Hanks in *Dragnet*. All kinds of weird *Nightmare* merchandise was marketed throughout the country: you could find pinball machines, Freddy Krueger action figures, talking dolls, posters, comic books, plastic knife finger gloves, squirting Freddy heads, board games, calendars, playing cards, and decals. I would even eventually stumble upon a Freddy Krueger pillbox sold in a kiosk at Catherine the Great's summer palace while on location in St. Petersburg, Russia. In Cyrillic on this unlicensed (sorry, New Line) sleeping-pill/Valium container next to Freddy's likeness, it read, "Take one and he'll come for you."

CHAPTER
8

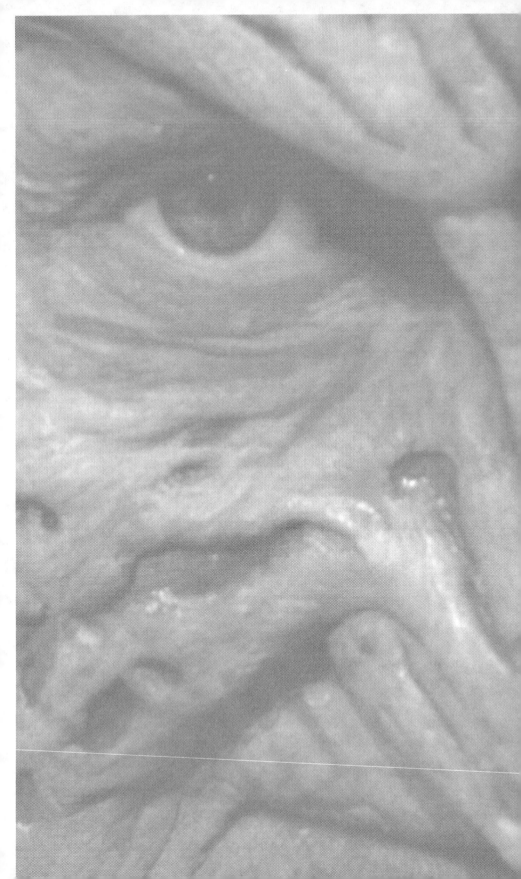

NIGHTMARE #8:

I'm on a rocky promontory surrounded by boulders baking in the hot sun. A childhood friend is trapped above me. I'm climbing down to get help, and my foot gets wedged in a crevice. I pry it out and resume my descent down the steep cliff toward a dead tree jutting from the stone. I reach a drop-off and can go no further. I try to climb back up to the dead tree. I'm stuck. I keep trying to climb down with no success. The frightening recurring image in the dream is a vertiginous look over the edge of the cliff. It's dizzying and nauseating, like Jimmy Stewart on the stairs of the bell tower in Alfred Hitchcock's *Vertigo*. It's been a long time since I suffered through this nightmare. But not long enough.

*N*IGHTMARE 3 RAKED IN A WHOPPING $45 million, so come 1988, New Line of course commissioned a sequel to the sequel of the sequel. Again demonstrating an uncanny eye for new talent, Bob Shaye discovered three young screenwriters who would together come up with a different twist for Freddy and his victims.

An untried twenty-seven-year-old wunderkind, Brian Helgeland launched his career in high style with *A Nightmare on Elm Street 4: The Dream Master*. Brian—who would go on to win an Oscar for his screenplay of *L.A. Confidential*, get nominated for his adaptation of *Mystic River*, and concoct such box-office monsters as *Conspiracy Theory* and *Payback*—demonstrated a keen sense of structure that would make him one of Hollywood's highest-paid writers. Writing under the pseudonym of Scott Pierce, brothers Jim and Ken Wheat had a modicum of experience, but compared to Brian, they were practically grizzled veterans. Their first feature film was a 1980 sci-fi flick called *The Return*, which featured one of the odder casts you'd ever want to meet at a sci-fi fest: Martin Landau, Cybill Shepherd, Raymond Burr, Neville Brand (from Tobe Hooper's *Eaten Alive*), and my old friend and co-star Jan-Michael Vincent. Five years later, they codirected and cowrote a *Star Wars* spin-off TV movie for ABC called *Ewoks: The Battle for Endor*. I had auditioned for the original *Ewok*

Adventure with Kitty Winn from *The Exorcist*. Neither of us got the part. Too young again.

I think the reason so many young creatives—and I don't mean only writers, but also directors, cameramen, and special effects techs—gravitated to the *Nightmare* franchise and were willing to work for low pay was because these movies offered them a real chance to stretch. More so than in a television series, or a romantic comedy, or a straight low-budget indie flick, they could really show off, strut their stuff as long as they stayed within the budget of their department. Taking creative chances was not only accepted, but also encouraged. The dream sequences were particularly fertile ground because they gave people the opportunity to let their imaginations fully flower. Wes Craven and Bob Shaye had never been meddlesome backseat drivers. Once they hired you, they trusted you to deliver. They gave advice but weren't always second-guessing you. Another plus was that although New Line paid you peanuts on your first gig, if you did a good job, they promised to hire you to work on other New Line projects. The next time out, you'd likely get a bump in pay and so on. They were true to their word; the minimum-wage interns on the first *Nightmare* were in the camera department by *Nightmare 4* and could now afford a down payment on a house, drive cars that didn't break down every four blocks, and even start families.

Taking advantage of the opportunity to spread their wings on *Nightmare 4*, Brian Helgeland et al. let it rip. For the first time in the franchise the three writers picked up the story more or less where the last *Nightmare* left off.

I'd been working my ass off on the series *Downtown*, so when the filming for *Nightmare 4* started, I was beat. As tough as a movie shoot can be, it's far less difficult than a weekly sixty-minute episodic drama with multiple locations. Television hours are a real grind; you're always adapting to changing conditions and the commutes suck. (Tyne Daly had the right idea when she was on *Cagney & Lacey*: when the schedule became too grueling, she would sometimes sleep in the studio car overnight at the next location, which gave her time to learn her dialogue for the following day. By minimizing the schlepping back and forth, she gained precious hours of sleep and was able to deliver Emmy Award–winning work on an insane timetable.) On the other hand, television money was far better than movie money—I'll take a *V* paycheck over an early *Nightmare* one anytime.

As had become the rule, another *Nightmare* meant another hot new director, and, boy, did we find a good one, a talented foreigner with a vision, Renny Harlin. A blond giant from Finland, Renny had already directed two films, one of which was *Prison*, a tight little ghost thriller that starred an unknown Viggo Mortensen. Rumor had it that during our shoot Renny hadn't had time to find a place to stay in Hollywood yet, so he crashed on his agent's couch. I've always liked that image: this big guy who went on to direct the megablockbusters *Die Hard 2* starring Bruce Willis, *Cliffhanger* starring Sylvester Stallone, and *Deep Blue Sea* starring Samuel L. Jackson, curled up on the sofa like a husband banished from the bedroom.

Coming off months of long hours and rush-hour commutes on my weekly series *Downtown*, I was feeling like dog meat and certainly wasn't thrilled with the idea of getting back in that fucking makeup chair and facing cold glue and those stiff makeup brushes every morning. I was dragging ass, and Renny, to his credit, realized it. In hindsight, you have to be impressed that the guy was perceptive enough to notice that even though the performance was okay, his star wasn't inspired.

Renny was hip to all kinds of new technology, most impressively a piece of equipment called video assist. It's pretty much exactly what it sounds like: you take your video assist unit, attach it to the top of a camera, let it run simultaneously with the movie camera, then, once the scene is over, you can watch what you'd just shot from the exact same camera angles. Today, with digital film, that probably sounds antiquated, but back then, we thought it was pretty damn cool. Renny was a big fan of video assist and generally watched the shooting from behind an enclosed monitor rather than next to the camera.

Some of the shoot took place in the northeast end of the Valley, a sprawling area of extremely variable weather. It can be scorching during the day, then, once the sun sets, it can drop down to near freezing. The Universal Studios backlot is infamous for plummeting temperatures and ground fog. One Friday night we were out in the Valley, shooting the junkyard sequence, and it was getting colder and a damp wind was picking up. I was still alert enough to recognize that the set was phenomenal, as spectacular as any set I'd worked on. They'd stacked old wrecks ten high to form a canyon of junked cars, and when the headlights magically blinked on like evil eyes, it looked like a junkyard from hell. Where else would Freddy and his crazy mutt hang out?

Around three in the morning, between takes, I was slouched in my director's chair wrapped up in a wardrobe blanket, shivering. Renny loped over and said, "Robert, c'mere. I wanna show you something."

"A hot-coffee enema? An Irish coffee laced with Bushmills? Anything would be better than the mud they've been serving us for the past two weeks."

"Even better. Check it out." Renny is well over six feet tall, and at the time he had long blond hair, halfway to his ass. He looked like a fucking Viking, and when a Viking asks you to follow him, you follow him, no matter how cold or tired you may be.

He led me over to the video assist playback machine and fired it up. He and his editors had slapped together a rough cut of everything in the junkyard sequence that had been shot up to that point. Huddled like some monster monk with a blanket over my bald head, teeth chattering, clutching a craft-services cup-a-soup for warmth, I stood transfixed, watching what they'd come up with. It was original, stylish, full of camera movement and jump cuts, and it was enough to give a freezing Freddy a second wind. I don't know how he knew I needed that, but that little glimpse of assembled footage got my adrenaline rushing big-time. Renny's sneak peek motivated me through my toughest *Nightmare* shoot yet.

A couple days later, we headed to Pacoima, again out in the north Valley. For the first time in *Nightmare* history, Freddy Krueger was going to be seen in the light of day. All of our previous outdoor filming had been at night, but our writers had contrived a dream with Freddy at the beach, so it was off to . . . Hansen Dam?

Hansen is a large, once bucolic body of water now a little worse for wear and a bit forlorn that's been around since the 1930s, regularly used for Hollywood locations, a recent example being 2003's *Charlie's Angels: Full Throttle*. A golf course was nearby, as well as an aquatic center, a full-blown recreation area, horseback-riding trails, and a historical museum. It's also the neighborhood where Rodney King got his ass kicked. What better place for Freddy to make his outdoor debut?

In the scene we were shooting that day, Kristen Parker, who, this time out, was being played not by Patricia Arquette, but rather by a vivacious blond singer/actress named Tuesday Knight—and, yes, Tuesday Knight is her real name—falls asleep on the beach and has a dream in which a shark fin pops up from the water, then turns into a claw, which, of course, announces the arrival of our Mr. Krueger. Freddy then slinks out of the water wearing his usual Freddy garb, augmented only by a pair of Ray-Ban sunglasses. Even Freddy has a fashion sense. Having grown up a surfer, I was comfortable around the water . . . but, of course, I'd never jumped into a lake while dressed up as a claw-wielding psychopath.

The producers arranged to have a special trailer for me where Howard Berger, an inventive makeup artist who would go on to win an Oscar in 2005 for *The Chronicles of Narnia*, could apply the Freddy makeup FX. As this was the fourth *Nightmare*, getting in my makeup had become second nature to me. It was tedious and often uncomfortable, but it came with the proverbial territory. However, my monster had never really seen the sun, and I suspected that it might be a problem for him . . . or, actually, me. My trailer was air-conditioned, so I was comfortable while Howard was doing his thing, but I knew that once I left the cool interior climate—once my makeup and I got a taste of the ninety-degree day outside— my comfort would be kaput.

After Howard successfully applied the Freddy face, I took

a tentative step outside, and almost immediately my brain started boiling like an egg yolk. I was as hot as I'd ever been on a set, and that's including the time I'd done my first fire stunt on *Nightmare 2*. But I was a professional, so I looked at the fake palm trees and the augmented, art-department beach sand, savored my last moment of air-conditioning, strode into the blistering heat, and commenced the business of scaring the shit out of Tuesday.

We finished the scene in just under three hours, and those three hours were tough for everybody on both sides of the camera. As if my boiling brain and the Freddy makeup slowly filling up with sweat weren't misery enough, the Santa Ana winds kicked up, blowing Hollywood sand everywhere, ruining Tuesday's hairstyle and making it nearly impossible for our soundmen to get a clean take of our dialogue.

Then there were the uninvited guests. Hundreds of them.

I was so wrapped up in getting the scene in the can without passing out face-first in the reservoir from heat prostration that I didn't notice the huge audience gathering until I was on my way back to the trailer to remove my makeup. Fifty yards from the beach set, a crowd of *Nightmare* fans had congregated to watch us film. Our security people had set up a cordon, but the natives seemed restless, and I wasn't optimistic that it would hold.

The crowd screamed for me to come over and sign autographs, and normally I would've been happy to do so, but I was dehydrated and exhausted, and I was afraid that if I didn't get out of my makeup *immediately*, my head would explode. I gave them a wave, a smile, and an apology, then headed into the trailer.

Howard realized how miserable I was, so he dived right in. He'd removed about half of the makeup when suddenly a dull thud came on the side of the trailer. Then another one. And another. Howard cautiously separated the trailer's venetian blinds and took a quick peek out the window. Turned out I was right—the cordon hadn't held. Scores of fans were surrounding the trailer, pounding on the sides, chanting, "Fred-*DEE,* Fred-*DEE,* Fred-*DEE!*"

Stunned, Howard turned and said, "They really want your autograph, Robert. You better go out there, or they're never going to leave."

I stood up with half my makeup still hanging off my face and sighed. "Fine, I'm going." I grabbed a Sharpie from my backpack and readied myself to sign an autograph or ten. Or twenty. Or a hundred. Anything to keep me and Howard from getting trampled.

Thankfully, the crowd stopped pounding on the trailer the second I opened the door. As I signed bits of scrap paper, baseball hats, napkins, assorted body parts including two perfect biker chick breasts (Freddy Krueger's signature on one breast and Robert Englund's on the other—ha, my daddy didn't raise no fool), the fans applauded and continued their chant: "Fred-*DEE,* Fred-*DEE,* Fred-*DEE!*" I answered a few questions, posed for some quick snapshots, made a couple of scary faces, cackled the Freddy laugh, then lied, "My makeup man has to leave in ten minutes, and he's gotta get the rest of this stuff off. Thanks for coming, and look out for *A Nightmare on Elm Street Four: The Dream Master* coming soon to Hell's Octoplex!" Then, to hoots and applause, I went inside.

Almost immediately, the pounding started up again. Then

the makeup trailer began to rock. Howard said, "Oh, shit, we gotta get outta here. Pretty soon they're gonna tell their friends you're here, and you'll be signing autographs all night. Sit down. Let's finish this." He removed the rest of the makeup in record time, somehow managing not to scrape off my epidermis.

"Fred-*DEE*, Fred-*DEE*, Fred-*DEE!*"

The crowd was rocking the trailer back and forth. I don't know whether they wanted me to come back out, or if they just wanted to flip the trailer over. This would have made a great scene in *Wes Craven's New Nightmare:* the monster and the villagers, updated!

Panicked, I looked at Howard. He stared back, scared. "We have to get the fuck out of here. *Now!*" I shouted.

Howard said, "I'll go first. You get behind me. I'll run interference." He gulped. "Ready?"

"Ready."

"Okay. One . . . two . . . three . . . *go!*"

He somehow got the door open with one shove. The crowd parted, assuming I was coming out to sign more stuff. They assumed wrong. Howard and I fought our way through the mass of bodies, then sprinted toward the parking lot, where we split off to our respective vehicles. The crowd sprinted right after us. Despite the heat and my exhaustion, I ran as fast as I'd ever run in my life and put some distance between me and the Freddymaniacs.

My car was a three-year-old cherry 5.0 Mustang convertible. Fortunately I'd left the top down, so I vaulted over the front seat, jammed the key in the ignition, and shifted into reverse. I couldn't take off the way I wanted to because, after all,

I was in a parking lot, so my pursuers were able to stay with me as I drove toward the exit. Eventually, I shook them and made it safely onto the freeway.

Or so I thought.

Two minutes later, an old, beat-to-hell Dodge Dart drew even with me on my driver's side. The car's driver laid on the horn, opened his window, and stuck his smiling face out. "Yo, Freddy," the kid yelled, "why'd you take off so quick? Where you goin', man? Let's hang!"

I floored it. The Dart pulled behind me into my lane and got right on my tail. Then another car—a Mustang, almost identical to mine—joined the chase. As did a Harley-Davidson with a passenger, the girl whose breasts I'd signed.

Now, I'm not a reckless driver, but I can handle myself behind the wheel when necessary, so for the next ten minutes or so I dodged between cars, trucks, and motorcycles, trying to ditch my growing vehicular entourage. I was pretty confident I'd lost my little parade, but to play it safe, I shot past my exit, then took a circuitous route back to my house and hid my car in the garage, just in case anyone was still following me. Because if the fans found out where I lived, well, Freddy would've become the stalkee, not the stalker.

Since the script for *Nightmare 4* was so loaded with SPFX and our budget was only $13 million (which sounds like a lot, but for a movie like this, it wasn't, not even back then), we had several splinter units shooting simultaneously. Our soundstage was an old, converted industrial warehouse beyond the Valley, way the hell out in Santa Clarita. As of this writing, Santa Clarita has become one of the busiest film-production centers in southern California—in fact, *CSI* has called it home for ten seasons—but back then, it had mostly been used for old westerns and car chases. And as was the case over at the Hansen Dam, it was hotter than hell out there.

One day, I had to drag my ass out of bed at four in the morning so I could be on the set for a 5 a.m. makeup session. By the time I got out to Santa Clarita, it was nearing eighty degrees . . . and this was before the sun came up. As was usually the case with these early calls, my makeup crew and a few on-set painters were the only people at the stage. One of the art-department girls was on her knees outside, drawing a hopscotch pattern on the sidewalk with a piece of colored chalk. She wasn't there to challenge anyone to a game; the crude drawing was actually for a scene in the movie, a child's graffiti warning that Freddy was coming. I was still half-asleep, so I didn't realize for a few seconds that we actually *weren't* the only people on the set that morning. A couple of cameramen on the other side of the soundstage were finishing up some inserts that they hadn't managed to get in the can the previous evening. It was a round-the-clock *Nightmare*.

THE SECOND, THIRD, AND fourth units got the shaft when it came to on-set chow. During the overnight shoots, craft services would be long gone, and these poor, hardworking folks would be stuck with lukewarm coffee, cold, gelatinous pizza fused to the cardboard of the take-out boxes, peanut-butter-and-jelly sandwiches crawling with flies, and if they were lucky, the remains of a jumbo economy bag of crushed

Cheetos. This graveyard shift was a skeleton crew composed of loyal, devoted Freddy fans, willing to forgive the late hours and craft-services leftovers in order to contribute their talents to the *Elm Street* experience.

Another entrée from the craft-services menu that nobody wanted to eat was our animatronic pizza, a robot pie in which all the toppings were the faces of Freddy's prior victims. Instead of a pepperoni slice or a meatball, imagine substituting the tiny, animated face of one of the film's teenagers. We were there all night trying to get the FX pizza to work right when somebody in the grip department told the first assistant director that his crew was starving and wondered if they could order some food. The AD grinned and said, "Sure. Order up some pizza." The grips rang up Domino's and told them to rush over with a dozen large pizzas with the works.

Twenty-nine minutes and fifty-nine seconds later, a Domino's car pulls up to the set and out trudges the unfortunate soul stuck working the late-night runs. The guy had long dirty hair stuffed under a Domino's baseball cap, adolescent acne, and would rather have been anywhere else than a Santa Clarita industrial park delivering crap pizza in the middle of the night. This kid was slackerism personified.

While our production manager paid the kid, one of the FX crew guys sidled up to me and said, "Check this out." He had a little twinkle in his eye that hinted, *I'm up to no good.*

He then opened one of the pizza boxes, removed the Domino's pizza, replaced it with our animatronic death pie, and called the delivery boy over.

"Hey, fella, something's not right with this one. C'mere."

The kid shuffled over. "S'up, dude?"

"I don't know. There's something very weird going on here."

Then . . . our killer pizza came to life! The expression on that kid's face was priceless. It took us about fifteen minutes to stop laughing. I believe that somewhere there's a faded Polaroid of that moment. I'd love to see it. Domino's Slacker meets Robo-pizza. Classic.

It's been said that style-wise, *Nightmare 4* was the "MTV *Nightmare.*" In 1988, music videos were all the rage, and their jump-cut editing paradigm was influencing the look of commercials, mainstream television, and cinema. This new look meshed with the surrealistic dreamscape that Wes had originally created and worked perfectly as a design concept for *Dream Master.* Although our movie only cost $13 million, it looks as though we spent five times as much. Renny Harlin knew how to make one hell of a horror movie. He gave the film great bang-for-the-buck production value, kinetic action sequences, and a unique, unsettling, edgy feel. The first time I saw it, my initial thought was *Man, if you're into Freddy, watch* Nightmare 3 *and* Nightmare 4 *back-to-back and you've got the definitive Krueger double bill.*

Nightmare 4 contains my favorite sequence in the entire franchise, and I'm not even in it! Alice is locking up for the night at the Crave Inn diner—get it? . . . Crave Inn? . . . Craven? . . . Wes Craven? . . . Weren't we clever?—then she and Rick walk out to his truck, open the doors, and get in, and then . . . the sequence repeats . . . and repeats and repeats in a time-disorienting, continuous loop. The first time I saw it, I was spooked because it reminded me of how my nightmares tended to function. That repeating exit was the most hypnotic, disturbing, and accurate depiction of a dream I'd ever seen.

Renny Harlin had found a way to unnerve even me, a jaded horror actor, and I couldn't help but be impressed. I think I realized then and there that playing Freddy Krueger would probably haunt me all the way to my obituary column, but I had finally made my peace with being identified as the logo character for the *A Nightmare on Elm Street* series. I was proud to be part of this burgeoning phenomenon.

Several years earlier, my old pal Mark Hamill had been feeling a bit typecast, concerned that his entire career might consist of reprising Luke Skywalker or other sci-fi–related roles. I'm sure he was being offered a ton of space-opera scripts of varying quality. Mark was a huge Mel Brooks fan, and at the time, both were top talents on the 20th Century Fox lot. Apparently Mel heard through the studio grapevine about Mark's dilemma, so he invited him up to his office for a chat. After some pleasantries, Mel told Mark, "Listen to me, kid—when you're lucky enough to have a hit character like Luke Skywalker, you embrace it. Enjoy. When you're on the merry-go-round, you don't get off until it stops turning." When I first heard the story, I didn't pay much attention. But now, with the success of the *Nightmare* franchise taking on a life and momentum of its own, I realized I was probably going to reprise Freddy as many times as New Line asked. Just like that continuous loop, the repeating-dream roundelay outside the Crave Inn from *Nightmare 4*, I was on the merry-go-round now. And that advice Mel Books gave Mark Hamill years before made perfect sense to me.

* * *

I'M NOT SURE HOW Wes felt about the entire end product; I do know however that he believed we went a little overboard with some of the humor—e.g., when Freddy turns Debbie into a cockroach, then spits the Roach Motel tagline in her face: "You can check in, but you can't check out." On the first *Nightmare,* the humor that existed wasn't very overt; most of the laughs were gallows humor born out of discomfort. But by *Nightmare 4,* more funny stuff was in the script, and I was quick to improvise a joke or two on the set myself.

Our editors can also take some blame for too many wisecracks; when they were given two different takes of the same scene, it seems they gravitated toward the more comedic rather than the darker option. These Freddy punch lines were used as a kind of punctuation mark, a way to end scenes with a filmic rim-shot. Had we kept Fred Krueger strictly the incarnation of pure evil, things might've become boring and predictable, but we also had to be careful that we didn't turn him into a Catskills comic.

Whatever we were doing, it worked; the fans approved. *Nightmare 4* made $50 million. As Freddy famously told one of his victims, "Welcome to prime time, bitch!" And prime time meant I had opportunities come my way that I'd never dreamed, including the chance to direct my first movie.

My agent, Joe Rice, had an old UCLA friend named Rhet Topham. Rhet had come up with a horror script that was built around the current ubiquitous 976 phone-sex toll numbers (e.g., 976-FUUK or 976-LUVV, where it would cost you a buck a minute to get your rocks off), which were a fad back in the eighties. The movie was called *976-EVIL,* and as its premise, posed the question "What if you called a 976 number, and the guy who answered the phone tried to recruit you to murder, maim, and pillage? And what if that guy was Satan?" Joe asked if I wanted to direct. I'd never imagined that my directorial debut would be with a horror flick, but I guess it made a certain sense, because not only was I familiar with the world of horror filmmaking, but I was comfortable in it. Plus my newly accrued horror-genre status would help put asses in the seats.

I called in a favor, and Kevin Yagher agreed to oversee the special effects makeup on the film. Once again Kevin and his crew went above and beyond the call of duty and on a limited budget created incredibly memorable design. Our star, Stephen Geoffreys, was gradually transformed from a sexually repressed innocent into a horrific incarnation of teenage lust and revenge. Stephen had already achieved cult status as Evil Ed in 1985's hit horror flick *Fright Night;* he'd also essayed a tragic performance alongside Sean Penn and Chris Walken in *At Close Range.*

Sandy Dennis was our female lead, and she certainly brought class to our production. She had won an Oscar in 1967 for her supporting role in *Who's Afraid of Virginia Woolf?* and was a seasoned professional who had a great sense of humor that she brought to the role of the fanatically religious Aunt Lucy. The film did well enough that four years later, a sequel was in production.

Casting can be difficult for me because having been on the other side of the desk I have too much empathy for the actors auditioning. It's especially tough when people come in, nail the audition, and I have to tell them thanks but no thanks because they just don't have the right look for the part, just like all those times when I was told I was too young or too old for the role. The actual shooting can be a pain sometimes too because as director you are always watching the clock.

My favorite part of moviemaking is postproduction. Even though it can be frustrating, I love editing. I love the freedom to juxtapose scenes that heretofore I thought had been locked in chronology on the page; I learned that shuffling sequences editorially sometimes enhances the narrative or provides mystery. You realize during editing that it is truly the most creative aspect of filmmaking. You can play with time, stretch moments, condense scenes, discover new rhythms. You can highlight good performances, correct and minimize weak ones. Editing is as close to playing God as you can get in filmmaking.

Even more than editing, I love playing with the postproduction sound mix. A strategically placed mournful train whistle, chirping birdsong, the hissing of sprinklers, an infant's wail . . . the perfect music cue can bring to life a flat scene and make it resonate in a way that you could never have imagined when you were on the set.

Directing has other advantages too. My set decorator on *976-EVIL*, Nancy Booth, was a mixture of a young Lauren Bacall and a teenage Amy Irving, with a bit of Ava Gardner tossed in for spice. I needed a pretext to spend more time with her, but I didn't want to risk a sexual-harassment suit, so I concocted a way to legitimately be around her. I would ask her to scout locations with me. Thing is, I'd already locked up the majority of my locations, but she didn't know that and was happy to drive me out to East Bumfuck and check out, say, the locker room in an abandoned high school. I would also use any excuse to visit her in the art department office—

anything from trying to match a paint swatch to borrowing some yogurt from her minifridge—just so I could see her or hear her laugh. One day I walked into the office and she was curled up under her desk, napping like a puppy. I sat down and stared at her for a half hour. Thank God she didn't wake up or she would probably have thought I was a perv.

After copious flirting, Nancy and I went out on our first official date during postproduction. At the end of the evening, we stood in the alley behind an old Hollywood screenwriters bar and had our first kiss. My knees practically buckled. I felt as if I were fourteen years old all over again. Having been through a failed marriage and a couple of serious relationships, I knew at that moment, after one kiss, that I was in love again. As James Garner said to Sally Field in *Murphy's Romance*, I also realized, "I was in love for the last time." When I expressed that to Nancy, she said, "All right. Get rid of your baggage, and call me." I did. And a few months later, we were engaged.

976-EVIL wasn't the best movie I've ever been associated with, but in the grand scheme of things it may be the most important. Had I not signed on to do that project and watched a sleeping girl lie, I wouldn't have met the love of my life.

CHAPTER 9

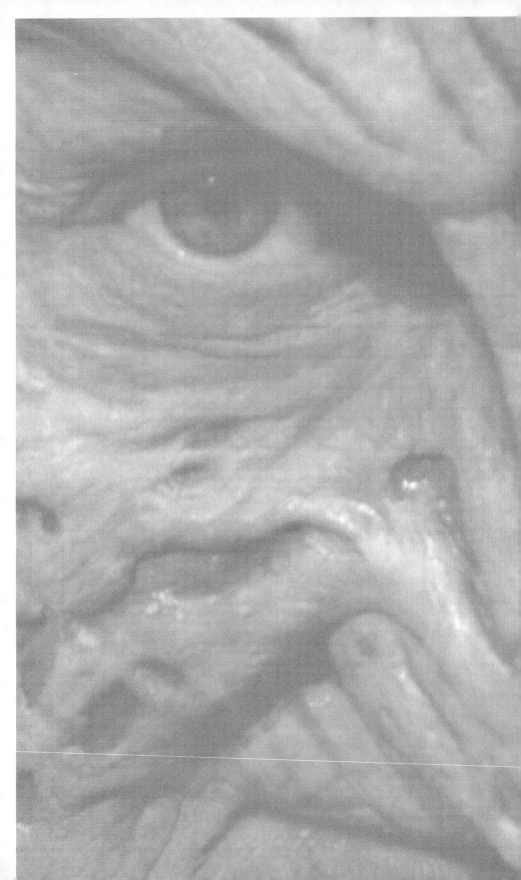

NIGHTMARE #9:

I've lived in a number of houses and apartments, and I've always had a plan for escape in case of intruders or fire. Since I was an athlete in my youth, I was comfortable that some of these escape routes involved jumping from second stories; I always felt secure and confident that I could save myself and rescue whichever girlfriend I was living with at the time. As the years passed and my old sports and stunt injuries began to take their toll on my body, I felt less sure of my ability to help my partner, or even to save my own sorry ass. These doubts and frustrations of old age have manifested themselves in recent years as a stress nightmare in which my home is invaded by hooded men or a fire has broken out downstairs. I find myself trapped on the roof or unable to hold on to my wife as I try to lower her safely from the eaves. I wake up soaked with night sweat.

THE *NIGHTMARE* MOVIES WERE UNDENIABLY popular in the United States, but over in Europe the fans couldn't get enough of Freddy either. I did a lot of publicity in major American cities, and I spent a good chunk of my downtime across the pond, hyping Freddy as well, which didn't leave much time for interviews and auditions. Pressing the flesh was fun, especially in London, Rome, and Paris, but I itched to act again. Even though I was pooped from the publicity junkets, I missed the set. Then, out of the blue, Renny Harlin called and said he was directing another movie, and he needed an actor who could replace Billy Idol. Billy had been in a motorcycle accident, and would I consider taking over at such short notice? So I replied in my best faux cockney, "Right-o guv'nah. Where do I bloody sign then?"

Renny's new project was *The Adventures of Ford Fairlane*, a star vehicle for up-and-coming comic Andrew Dice Clay. Andrew had a broad act—over-the-top vulgarity embodied in the persona of a Long Island stud. (Think *Happy Days'* Fonzie crossed with Buddy Love from *The Nutty Professor*.) *Ford Fairlane* was a new-wave rock-and-roll-cum-detective flick tailored to capitalize on Andrew's popular stand-up comedy act. It was a risky idea to exploit his fifteen minutes of fame, but if anybody could pull off this comedy hybrid, it was the tag team of Renny Harlin and Joel Silver.

Figuring that Andrew would have trouble carrying an entire movie, the producers brought together Wayne Newton, Priscilla Presley, Ed O'Neill, Gilbert Gottfried, Morris Day, Sheila E from Prince's band, and Mötley Crüe's Vince Neil to help out, which nudged the kitsch-o-meter into the red zone. With this bizarre collection of talent, we probably weren't going to win the SAG Award for Best Comedy Ensemble, but if all the stars aligned properly, I thought this might find an audience beyond Dice's rabid fan base.

I played a hit man/roadie, which involved some physical work—no fire stunts, thank God—so they found me a stunt double. Now I've had a number of stuntmen stand in for me on past movies, but never one before who looked so much like me as my double on *Ford Fairlane*. The resemblance was so uncanny that people would walk up to him at the craft-services table and ask him for my autograph.

The French stuntman would respond, *"Pourquoi?"* then grin and regale them with tales of his life as a stuntman/jazz musician/kickboxer. (He'd been a champion kickboxer, and rumor had it that he had once beaten the crap out of a young Jean-Claude Van Damme in an exhibition.) As a European accustomed to clean air and clear water, he was more than a little reluctant when it came time for him to double me in my big fight scene, which was to be filmed down in San Pedro, a cesspool otherwise known as the Port of Los Angeles. The script called for me to kickbox with the star in a sinking boat, and my stunt double wanted nothing to do with it. Renny was exasperated with the guy and called upon all of his persuasive powers to get him in the water. No go. Stubborn fuckin' frog.

I knew we were up against the wall time-wise, and they weren't about to go searching for another Robert Englund look-alike. So to preserve the integrity of my fight scene, I told Renny, "Listen, Pepé Le Pew over there is a great guy, but a bit of a pussy. Me, I'm an old surfer, I'll get in the goddamn water. Hell, I've been in worse." Turned out, I hadn't been in worse. Frenchy was right. I should've played the pussy card myself because that was the smelliest, most vile, disgusting body of water I've ever been in in my life. I saw things floating around me that were X-rated. Thankfully my dip in the harbor didn't leave me glowing in the dark. I haven't checked my sperm count.

Ford Fairlane had a decent budget, so we got to work at some great L.A. locations such as Malibu Beach, but my favorite was the iconic Capitol Records building in downtown Hollywood. As much fun as it was to float around in L.A. harbor with Dice Clay and Gilbert Gottfried, hanging out with Wayne Newton and Priscilla Presley in the very building where Frank Sinatra laid down some of the greatest vocal tracks of the twentieth century really appealed to my inner Rat Packer. Wayne Newton's reputation is that of a schmaltzy lounge singer, but few people know that Wayne has an encyclopedic knowledge of rock 'n' roll and is an accomplished guitar player as well. I loved grilling him for stories about Jackie Gleason, Ed Sullivan, Johnny Carson, old-school Las Vegas, and his friendship with Elvis Presley. His music-industry and showbiz gossip were as compelling as Henry Fonda's tales of old Hollywood, and a fascinating way to pass the time between takes.

* * *

FAST-FORWARD TO THE FOLLOWING year. My agent, Joe Rice, and I are on the *Ford Fairlane* press junket, headed off to Las Vegas to attend a roast of Joel Silver, the wildly successful and prolific producer who's midwifed such movie franchises as *Lethal Weapon, Die Hard,* and *The Matrix*. We were flown to Vegas on a private studio jet—accompanied by my old costars Johnny Depp and Jeff Bridges, along with Winona Ryder, Anjelica Huston, and CEO Barry Diller. If that puddle jumper went down, Hollywood was going to be out some big box-office bucks.

When we got to the hotel where we were going to tear Joel a new one, Wayne, Priscilla, and I walked through the casino together, and I had the quintessential showbiz moment. I was flanked by Mr. Las Vegas himself and the wife of the King of Rock 'n' Roll. They were Vegas royalty. The people parted as if we were demigods, some afraid to look Wayne and Priscilla in the eye, and some brave enough to ask one of them for an autograph or to blow on their craps dice for good luck. Between *V* and *Nightmare,* and attending dozens of movie premieres, I'd gotten a sense of what it's like to be a celebrity, but when Wayne Newton cruises through a casino in Vegas, that's CELEBRITY. It also gave me a curious sense of my place in show-business history at that moment; here I was in Sin City, hyping a contemporary nineties comedy, getting ready to roast a guy who'd played a key role in defining eighties popular cinema, and hanging out with icons from the sixties and seventies. It's not always easy being a Hollywood monster, but moments like that make all the bullshit worthwhile.

(A final note: *The Adventures of Ford Fairlane* made over

$20 million. Sometime later a controversy occurred between host Andrew Dice Clay and some of the female cast members on *Saturday Night Live*. It may just have been political correctness run amok, but it took the wind out of Dice's sails for a while. Since then, Andrew has resumed a successful career touring his stand-up comedy act, and returned to NBC with an ever-so-brief stint on *The Celebrity Apprentice*; and *Ford Fairlane* has been rediscovered and become a bona fide cult hit. *Fairlane* fans often accost me with Dice's favorite epithet for my character: "Yo, Snapperhead.")

European filmgoers had taken quite a liking to me, and so too had Menahem Golan. He offered me the lead in a remake of *The Phantom of the Opera*. One-half of the infamous Golan-Globus production team, Menahem had taken the Roger Corman business plan—use lower budgets to make more movies—to the max. (That said, I was handsomely paid. Corman would've committed hara-kiri before he'd sign off on my *Phantom* salary.) Prior to *Phantom*, Menahem Golan had produced, executive-produced, or had a hand in writing almost two hundred movies; afterward, he added another forty or so to his filmography. The guy knew how to get movies made.

Andrew Lloyd Webber's megahit musical version of *Phantom* had opened on the stage in 1986, and, come 1988, Menahem figured it would be a clever business move to make yet another film version. (Lon Chaney did it in 1925, then Claude Raines in 1943, then Herbert Lom in 1962, and Maximilian Schell in 1983. *Shit*, I thought, *I am going to be in good company*.) Menahem knew a filmed *Phantom* would attract fans of the hit Broadway musical, who would instantly recognize the title. Menahem also calculated that if he hired me, he could draw an audience from fans who loved me in *Nightmare* and were curious to see me in another horror-movie role. He wanted to exploit—and I don't mean "exploit" in a bad way, necessarily—my Freddy fame and turn me into a Vincent Price/Boris Karloff genre star. *Nightmare 5* was still in development, and I had nothing pressing on my docket, so it was off to Hungary.

The Budapest of 1988 was still chaffing under Soviet rule; it wasn't uncommon to see a fifteen-year-old Russian soldier leaning against a Belle Epoque lamppost and smoking a cigarette, a Kalashnikov slung over his shoulder, flirting with a local girl.

Christine, the female lead, was played by Jill Schoelen, fresh off the nifty little thriller *The Stepfather*, in which she costarred with Terry O'Quinn, who would eventually go on to fame and fortune as John Locke in *Lost*. She'd also recently shot a low-budget horror film with Brad Pitt called *Cutting Class*, as well as the musical *Babes in Toyland* with Keanu Reeves. (How about that? This old character actor shared a leading lady with two of *People* magazine's sexiest men alive.) Bill Nighy, who had yet to cross over from British stage star to international film star—can you say *Pirates of the Caribbean?*—was also along for the ride. The Phantom got to kill Bill, a classically trained Englishman whose work I'd always loved, in a Turkish steam bath, which was almost as much fun as killing Burt Reynolds.

Before filming began, our director, Dwight Little, and I had several conversations about how I should play the role, and the style of the movie. We decided to think of it as a reimagining, an homage to the classic Hammer Film productions.

Hammer was a UK company founded in 1935, which, twenty years later, became one of the leading exporters of fright flicks, e.g., *The Curse of Frankenstein, Dracula,* and *The Mummy.* With their rich, saturated color, Hammer films had a distinct look and often featured heavyweights such as Christopher Lee, Peter Cushing, and Oliver Reed. We wanted to bring a similar sense of class, style, and not-so-subtle sexuality to our version of *Phantom.* (The Hammer film that had the biggest impact on me was *Brides of Dracula,* a flick I caught at a drive-in movie. I was on my way to second base with my date, fumbling to unhook her bra, when out of the corner of my eye I saw the big-screen vampire bite a beautiful actress's neck. Then, as her warm blood coursed down her cleavage, she surrendered in Hollywood ecstasy to her fate. I was so entranced that I actually halted my pursuit of second base and watched the movie because, frankly, it was more of a turn-on.)

I was reunited with Kevin Yagher, my makeup man from *Nightmare 2* and *Nightmare 3* and *976-EVIL,* and as usual he outdid himself. As opposed to the Freddy makeup, which was foam latex prosthetics applied directly to my skin, Kevin's design here required him to apply makeup on top of makeup, because in our version of *Phantom,* Erik Destler (aka the Phantom) didn't use anything as pedestrian as that Broadway musical mask, preferring instead to flay the facial skin from his victims and sew it on top of his own deformed flesh. This enabled him to attend his beloved opera without drawing attention to himself. I suppose you could think of Erik Destler as a less ambitious seamstress than Jame "Buffalo Bill" Gumb from *The Silence of the Lambs.*

When the Phantom was in deformed mode, Kevin made it appear as if the dead skin was rotting off, which could be a bitch for continuity, but Kevin didn't care. When it came to how my "public" visage would look, patched together from my victims' faces, Kevin took a different, more subtle tack. He had worked with me so much that he knew what would look best on my face, and rather than turn me into a completely different person, he chose to exaggerate my natural looks. For instance, he gave me a slightly sharper jawline, a little bit more of a brow, and some more definition in my cheekbones; in the right light, I resembled a living bust of Beethoven. In contrast to the mutilated, deformed look, it was a heroic, romantic countenance. Close-ups, however, would reveal the ghoulish nip-and-tuck work of the demented composer Erik Destler. (Kevin, it should be noted, was juggling about six projects, so he didn't make the trip to Hungary with me, sending Everett Burrell, his right-hand man at the time, and a veteran of *Nightmare 3*.)

Hair was yet another complication. Freddy was simply bald, so all we needed was a skullcap covered with burn scars and the signature fedora, and we were good to go. Erik the Phantom, however, had a thick mane of hair, so one of Kevin's assistants constructed a beautiful hairpiece back at Kevin's lab in California. We couldn't afford to bring Kevin's hair-meister with us to Budapest, so the care and feeding of the wig was left up to local hire. Fortunately, the Hungarian hair team was composed of little old ladies who'd toiled for years in the wig department of the world-famous Hungarian State Opera in Budapest. Their expertise was such that Erik's hairpiece was a cakewalk for these skilled professionals.

We shot *Phantom* at an old studio outside Budapest. Often on the dawn drive through the countryside we would find ourselves behind nineteenth-century oxcarts lit with swinging lanterns making their way to the village market. It was magical and helped get me in character; we weren't in Kansas anymore. The underground chamber set that was home to Erik Destler evoked both terror and romance and was carved entirely from Soviet Styrofoam, the Russian counterpart to the spread-open Quarter-Pounder-boxes-and-milk-crate spaceship interiors that James Cameron had created on the cheap for *Galaxy of Terror*, seven years before. The problem was, in this movie, lit candles were going to be everywhere on the set, and mixing live fire and Styrofoam is *not* OSHA-approved. For instance, Erik's labyrinth beneath the opera house where he composes his music and courts Christine was entirely lit by candles, not to mention that the climax of the movie was to be a fiery conflagration that destroys Erik and his lair. In terms of movie fires, this was simple stuff, but when Styrofoam is involved, the danger is exponentially amped, because when that shit burns, things can get acrid, poisonous, and dangerously drippy. Even more frightening to me was the possibility that my artificial hair would go up in flames—maybe from a candle, or the fire in the finale—and I didn't know exactly what kind of material Kevin and his crew had used to make my hair, but I was pretty certain it wasn't fireproof. Since our entire fire-safety department consisted of a brigade of four overweight, chain-smoking Hungarians sharing two Soviet-era fire extinguishers and a single bucket of water, I watched my every step, played it safe, and survived the shoot without any new additions to my collection of Hollywood scars. I'd leave the burn wounds for Mr. Krueger, and as it turned out, he'd need them soon enough.

IN 1988, NEW LINE called me up and asked if I'd like to do a television series featuring Freddy Krueger as a host. Freddy would function as a sort of Rod Serling from Hell, and the show would contain some scary shit. I was initially skeptical about the project because I couldn't really see Freddy on TV. How much violence would we be able to get away with? What about the sexual subtexts? Would the network censors take kindly to child killing? If it was going to be watered down, what was the point? I was assured that since we were going to be syndicated late at night, we'd be able to push the envelope as far as we possibly could. TV taboos would be broken. Plus— and this was the clincher—I could direct some episodes. That all sounded pretty good, so I was in.

Tobe Hooper shot the pilot, which had a lot of material regarding Freddy's backstory, serving almost as a prequel to the original *A Nightmare on Elm Street*, which audiences had been clamoring for. I felt the pilot script really surpassed the expectations of our legions of fans. Another episode that stands out is "Killer Instinct," directed by Mick Garris, who became the go-to director for Stephen King adaptations to the screen. I was reunited with Mariska Hargitay for one episode, and halfway through the first season, newcomer Brad Pitt guest starred.

New Line was loyal to their *Nightmare* film crews, but they could only pay them so much, and as I've noted, unless you're on a big-time shoot, TV money is usually better than movie money. I was able to convince a lot of the *Nightmare* veterans from *Part 4* to segue into the TV series. *The Dream Master* and *Freddy's Nightmares* back-to-back meant a lot of overtime and finally some healthy bank accounts for my hardworking crew.

After a run of thirty-eight episodes, the series was canceled in 1990, and it was time to take stock. I'd been Freddy in four feature-length movies and close to fifty hours of syndicated television. *Man,* I thought, *that's a lot of Freddy.* The fact of the matter was, I was ready to hang up the claw.

CHAPTER 10

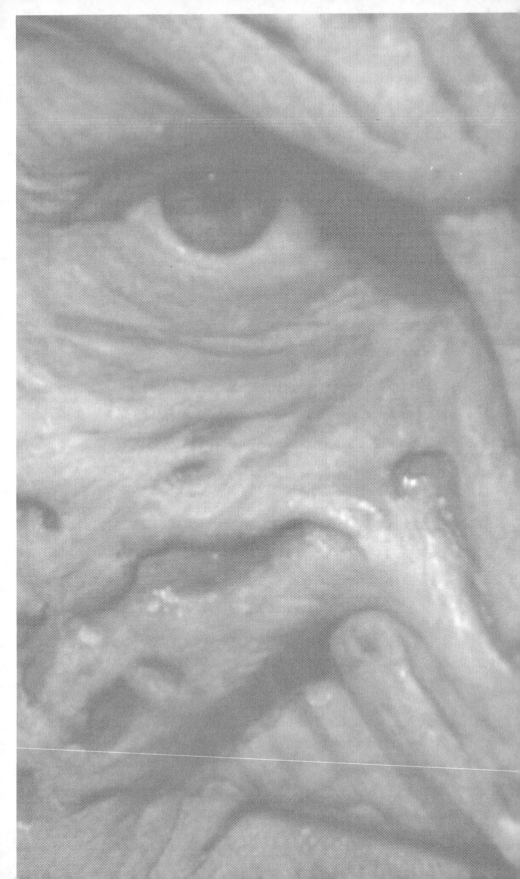

NIGHTMARE #10:

I was the kindergarten God of our jungle gym, a boxy structure with an elevated dome in the middle, and a fire pole running from the center of the dome to the sandbox below. I stood at the top watching friends slide down the pole, when suddenly one of my classmates slipped between the arched bars and fell all the way to the hard-packed sand, smashing into several of the horizontal framing bars on his way down. He had the wind knocked out of him and a nasty bump on his forehead; the lump swelled up so suddenly it looked like a cartoon goose egg. The egg remained for years, inspiring a cruel childhood nickname. Either advances in medical science or nature eventually cured Goose's affliction by the time we were in middle school. In my ensuing nightmare, my face is pressed against the cold steel pipes at the pinnacle of the jungle gym dome, and I watch as my friend falls in slow motion, and hear his head hit each steel bar on the way down.

I WAS FUCKING EXHAUSTED. PHYSICALLY, mentally, emotionally, and creatively, I was wiped. Anybody who'd abused himself with my schedule would've been.

Phantom had wrapped, and by now I'd shot close to forty episodes of *Freddy's Nightmares*. I needed a break; I mean, it's not as if I'd been on location in Hawaii guest-starring on *Magnum, P.I.* with a goddamn basket of fruit waiting for me back at the hotel. Nooooo, I'd been up to my ass in makeup behind the rusty Iron Curtain, surviving on a steady diet of goulash and Tokay.

So when I was approached to do *A Nightmare on Elm Street 5: The Dream Child,* I was on the fence. The thought of that uncomfortable makeup chair waiting for me, waking up every morning to latex Freddy boogers on my pillow, endless night shoots beating up my still jet-lagged body clock, and the obligatory soggy craft-services pizza was utterly unappealing. Actually, working *period* was unappealing to me; I had some movie and television offers on the back burner, but I was so fried that, for the first time in my Hollywood career, I considered taking a break and using some of my *Phantom* money to treat Nancy and myself to a romantic escape. Baja? No. Bali? Nah. Bob Shaye? Yes.

Bob pestered me to make a decision, but I couldn't and

wouldn't. I wasn't playing hard to get, nor was I trying to leverage a bigger salary—I didn't legitimately know whether I wanted to play Freddy again. This had nothing to do with me being tired of the character or the franchise or the horror genre. It was just about me being tired, period. But New Line, putting on the full-court press, sent me the script and begged me to meet with the latest gentleman who would sit in the *Nightmare* director's chair, Stephen Hopkins.

Born in Jamaica, Stephen's most impressive credential at that point was as assistant director on the Sean Connery vehicle *Highlander*, a film that began one of the more enduring fantasy franchises. I met Stephen at a Thai restaurant in Culver City, and the first thing that struck me was that this kid looked like a Hollywood leading man. *He should be in front of the camera*, I thought, *not behind it.* (And this is coming from a guy who worked with a young Jan-Michael Vincent and Johnny Depp.) After a steaming bowl of *tom ka kai*, Stephen pulled out a pen, grabbed a napkin, and started doodling, practically storyboarding the movie right in front of my eyes, and those rough drawings looked like the first draft of some kind of Freddy Krueger graphic novel. Not only was he movie-star handsome, but this guy could draw.

Stephen said, "There's one scene where I'd like to do an M. C. Escher sort of thing," then he illustrated an Escher-like sequence on the back of his place mat, and I was hooked. Just looking at his sketches, I was pretty confident I would be in good hands, and *The Dream Child* would be something unique.

(I know I have an eye for spotting acting talent, but, boy, did I get it right when I told the press that Stephen was going places. Of all our directors, he's arguably had the most impressive post-*Nightmare* career, having directed Michael Douglas and Val Kilmer in one of my favorite films, *The Ghost and the Darkness*, coproducing every episode from the premier season of *24* and directing half of them, and winning an Emmy for his work on one of the most original biopics you'll ever see, *The Life and Death of Peter Sellers*. And I called it. Thank you very much.)

As usual, a handful of writers worked on the screenplay, but I believe Leslie Bohem had the biggest hand in it. In 2002 he was the writer behind some ten episodes of Stephen Spielberg's *Taken*, for my money the best science fiction on television since *V*. Leslie and his writing team didn't have quite the firepower of the Frank Darabont/Bruce Wagner gang on *Nightmare 3*, but I believed enough in Stephen and his vision to go into the film with confidence.

Even though we had our biggest budget to date—a whopping $6 million—we shot in a funky building on the inland border of Venice, California. Surrounded by freeway off-ramps and encampments of the homeless, the production was housed in an old A-1 Spaghetti warehouse. On the plus side, it was right down the street from the best Cuban food in L.A., and only about twenty minutes away from my house. And thank God for that last part; after those brutal drives out to the high desert for *Nightmare 4*, the easy commute from my digs in Laurel Canyon was a blessing.

Again, the shooting schedule was exhausting, so most of the filming was a blur of makeup sessions and chasing our heroine, Lisa Wilcox, around the set. However, Stephen Hopkins's Escher-esque sequence did stand out. This complicated series of shots took us a couple of days to film, which, on a *Nightmare* movie, is a luxury. It was a bitch for me, however, because I had to hang upside down for the majority of the scenes. The crew was sympathetic to my plight, and every time Stephen called "Cut," three grips would sprint over, grab my back, and support me so the blood could flow out of my head and down into my lower extremities. The converted soundstage at the spaghetti warehouse was as hot as a real boiler room, and my makeup was extra-itchy and thus required more touch-ups than usual. Between the heat, the melting makeup, and spending far too much time with my toes pointed toward the ceiling, that was arguably one of my most difficult experiences on any of the *Nightmare* shoots. Whenever I think about it, I get the whirlies.

One of the more colorful, descriptive lines of dialogue used to reference Freddy's backstory was "Freddy Krueger, bastard son of a hundred maniacs," and in *Nightmare 5* we explored that poetic image. We went back in prequel time, and we got to see me as Fred Krueger's father, the maniac who in the backstory rapes little Fred's mommy-to-be, the nun Amanda, who has accidentally been locked in the asylum overnight. For that scene, the casting department recruited virtually every psycho-looking performance-art theater actor in Los Angeles, herded them all together inside the insane-asylum set with me, and locked the door.

Stephen wanted us to have as much freedom as possible to improvise within the confines of the crowded set, so he filmed using a remote-control camera crane. This meant no crew in the room. The inmates would be running the asylum. This was the first time I'd worked with one of those cameras, and the thrill of working alone without the crew right there, surrounded by drooling, wild-eyed actors, dancing with the camera, if you will, put Renny's video assist unit from *Nightmare 4* to shame. We'd rehearsed the choreographed camera moves seemingly forever, but when the camera finally floated around the room filming, it gave the sequence a dangerous, improvisatory, documentary feel that was as trippy and weird as any of our dream sequences.

Because this was my fifth film as Freddy, I'd developed what I believed to be an unerring instinct as to what was right and wrong for the character. At some point an actor actually knows more about his character than anybody else, except perhaps the original writer. This is especially true on long-running television series, where oftentimes cast members have to deal with guest directors who aren't that familiar with the show's characters. Directors may understand the style and formula of a particular show and be efficient visual storytellers, but actors acquire a sixth sense about what makes their characters tick and recognize when they are asked to do something that violates that character's reality. They know they have to protect and defend their character, and this effort by an actor can sometimes be misconstrued by producers and directors as selfish, vain, or egotistical behavior. It's not. It's actually what we're paid to know.

Even though *Nightmare 5* wasn't exactly the critics' favorite, and our domestic box office was slightly disappointing, New Line realized that the franchise would survive. By this time, video rental was a huge business, and now an entire generation who'd missed the *Nightmare* films in movie theaters was getting a chance to discover them at home. Which, fortunately for us, they embraced with all their good ol' American consumerism gusto. Kids of all ages would have *Nightmare* marathons, memorize the plots and the characters, and collect the multiplying Freddy-abilia being churned out by the growing merchandizing machine. My fan mail increased tenfold, and I could barely keep up. To help me, I drafted my wife, Nancy, whose actual given name has confused more than one fan over the years—if you'll recall, the lead character in *A Nightmare on Elm Street* was named Nancy—and she became the official Freddy Krueger aide-de-camp.

So for the record, I did not marry Heather Langenkamp. Or Nancy Thompson. Just regular ol' Nancy Englund. Get it? Got it? *Good!*

CHAPTER 11

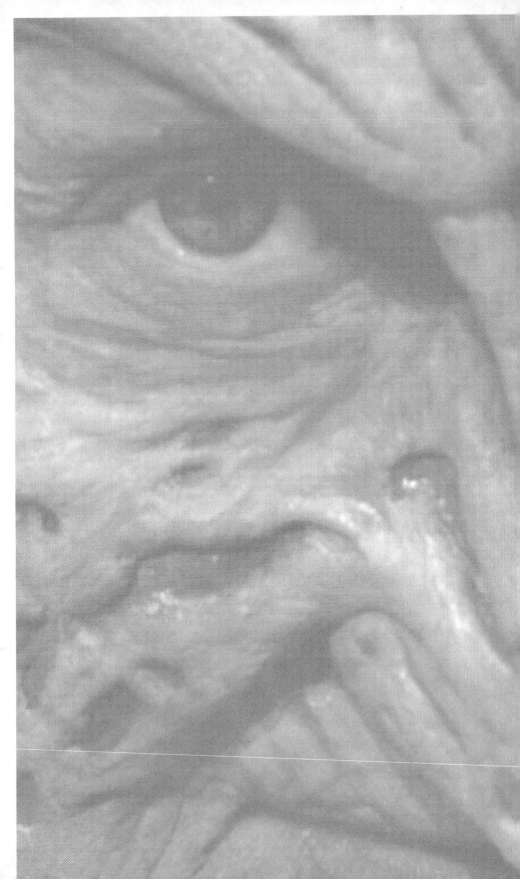

NIGHTMARE #11:

When I turned eight, I was assigned the very grown-up chore of riding my bike to the bakery and buying the family doughnuts. There was a certain freedom on those mornings, and I looked forward to the independence of my Saturday quest—until the morning I convinced a neighbor buddy to accompany me. Racing through a mid-century neighborhood on a shortcut to the bakery, we rounded a corner just in time to see our first dead bodies being covered by sheets; there had been a car accident and one paramedic was on the scene already. After we picked up the doughnuts, childhood curiosity got the best of us, and we returned home on the same route. By now, red Rorschach stains had started spreading beneath the sheets, an image that became stamped onto my subconscious forever.

S O, YES, I'D CARVED MYSELF A NICE LITTLE niche for myself in horror-movie history. Freddy had definitely wedged his boot in the door and was now mentioned in the same breath along with the famous monsters of filmdom: Frankenstein, Dracula, Wolf Man, and the Mummy . . . but that didn't stop us from killing him off. Truth be told, the time had come. It was 1991—almost seven years after Wes Craven had unleashed Mr. Krueger upon the unsuspecting moviegoing public—and most of the people involved with *Nightmare* thought, *You know what, enough is enough. But, hey, let's go out strong. Let's finish up with a bang.* The consensus was that if we were going to give Freddy a proper burial, we needed a radical departure from the rest of the series. The result was *Freddy's Dead: The Final Nightmare*: part Warner Bros. cartoon and part John Waters "camp." Warners and Waters is a movie I'd pay good money to see. If that's not going out with a bang, I don't know what is.

For the first time since the original *A Nightmare on Elm Street,* which Wes both wrote and directed, our new director had a hand in writing the screenplay too. But this wasn't just *any* novice auteur off the street—this was Rachel Talalay, who had been with us since the beginning and clawed her way up the ladder, all without even having to wear a goddamn glove. On the first *Nightmare,* she was an assistant production manager, which is a fancy way of saying she did whatever needed to be done, from reams of paperwork, to getting Wes a doughnut, to helping David Miller find the missing one-inch piece of foam rubber that had fallen off my ear while I was wrestling with Heather. On *Nightmare 2*, Rachel was a production manager, which meant that she could tell somebody else to get the director a doughnut or hunt for the fucking foam. On *Nightmare 3*, she was a line producer, which offered her a chance to be part of the creative process, although she probably had to shout to be heard. On *Nightmare 4*, she was an honest-to-goodness producer, which meant that people were getting her doughnuts. She handed the producing reins over to her husband, Rupert Harvey, for *Nightmare 5* while she produced John Waters's *Hairspray* and *Cry-Baby*, which might explain why there's such a Waters vibe about *Nightmare 6*.

In *Freddy's Dead*, we had the best *Nightmare* cameo performances since Zsa Zsa Gabor and Dick Cavett sparred with yours truly on that fake talk-show couch back in '87. The newlyweds Roseanne Barr and Tom Arnold made a brief appearance, as did rocker/actor/golf fanatic Alice Cooper as Freddy's sadistic stepfather. But the most offbeat cameo of all was the appearance of one Oprah Noodlemantra. If you looked closely at Mr. Noodlemantra during his brief scene, you'll notice that he bore a suspicious resemblance to the teenage male lead from the first *Nightmare*, one Johnny Depp.

A *Nightmare*-phile with a wicked sense of humor and a contemporary edge, Rachel pulled out all the stops: there's a cartoon sequence, a 3-D sequence, a black-and-white sequence, and a Freddy-goes-skateboarding sequence. Putting Freddy in day-to-day situations, having him do the kind of things that kids would do (e.g., playing video games), was our way of commenting on how Freddy had infiltrated pop culture. Plus, we simply wanted to have some fun; since day one, regardless of how hard everybody worked, we'd had a great time making the *Nightmare* films, and we were trying to get that sense of joy across to the audience.

To be 100 percent honest, I'll admit that on *Nightmare 6* we jumped the shark. (A quick tutorial on shark jumping: The phrase refers to a three-part episode of *Happy Days* in which the Fonz does a water-ski leap over a caged shark, which was just about the stupidest thing the Fonz could possibly have done. So when a TV or movie series jumps the shark, that means they've veered off into a direction that's detrimental to the original concept, the actors, and, most important, the viewers.) The comedy might've become a little too broad, the fantasy might've become a little too trippy, and the violence might've become a little too cartoonish. But in the grand scheme of things, we did pretty well, especially when you compare our series to other film franchises: *Lethal Weapon* jumped the shark the fourth time out, *The Godfather* lost it on number three, and don't even get me started about *The Phantom Menace.*

Apparently the Freddy freaks forgave us for the shark jumping: *Nightmare 6* grossed over $35 million, almost $10 million more than *Nightmare 5*. What with the good box office and the good reviews, we all felt it was safe to have Freddy call it a night. It was like saying good-bye to an old friend. A beat-to-shit, smelly, fashion-challenged, flesh-oozing, K-Y-jelly-covered old friend, but an old friend nonetheless.

I toasted Wes Craven and New Line Cinema and went about preparing for my post-*Nightmare* life. Step one: get a facial.

THE FOLLOWING YEAR, OUT of the blue, Wes called me and asked if I'd like to do a television series for NBC with him up in Vancouver. He explained that it would be similar to *The Twilight Zone*, in that each episode would take on a different subject matter or genre. Home base for the three leads was going to be a kind of purgatory, manifested in the form of an all-night diner, and he asked me to play one of the establishment's dead denizens. We were throwing around names like *Terminal Café* and *Last Chance Diner*, but the network was balking because they wanted the word "Nightmare" in the title to capitalize on the involvement of Wes and me. Wes settled for *Nightmare Café*, and the network was happy.

My character was named Blackie, a turn-of-the-century gambler, stranded in limbo, who served as a kind of night manager/gatekeeper at the diner, steering lost souls toward redemption. One of my costars was Jack Coleman, who then was best known for playing Steve Carrington on *Dynasty* and went on to star as Noah Bennet on *Heroes*. The best part was that Wes was on the set every day, offering suggestions, making changes, instantly correcting dialogue on the first laptop I'd ever seen, and, as always, punning incessantly. (Somehow Wes has kept his inner fourteen-year-old alive and well.) With its ever-changing themes and style—one week we'd shoot a

National Enquirer–like spoof about tabloid aliens, and the following week we were tugging at heartstrings with a serious dramatic story about an African-American family—the show was keeping me on my toes and I was loving it. We only shot six episodes, and I'll always be disappointed we didn't get to do sixty.

From the ahead-of-its-time opening title sequence, to the closing credits, and everything in between, *Nightmare Café* looked so goddamn good that it was held up as the new standard for production values on NBC. In terms of the variety of the stories we were telling, no other series remotely like us was on the air at that time. I'll admit that with its shifting styles and moods, and the only common denominator being the three stars in the diner, the show was a little hard to figure out. But had we stayed on the air, and had we been given a chance to grow, *Nightmare Café* might've achieved the status of Wes's other successful projects. With two original, quality TV series prematurely canceled out from under me, I was getting a little gun-shy about network television. If a good gig came along, I'd jump on it, but I wasn't going out of my way to get on the tube.

During the filming of our last episode, Wes approached me and casually mentioned, "So I've been talking with Heather."

"Langenkamp?"

"Yeah."

"About what?"

"About an idea I have to deconstruct the *Nightmare* phenomenon."

I had no clue what he was saying, but listening to Wes's ideas had always proved entertaining and fruitful. He continued, "I want to do a new *Nightmare* film where we all play ourselves and explore the effect the franchise's success has had on our lives and on the culture in general. We can satirize Hollywood, the horror genre, and scare the hell out of people at the same time."

That sounded like *Head* to me. In 1968, my *Stay Hungry* director, Bob Rafelson, had made a strange little movie in which he deconstructed the phenomenon he'd created, the prefab pop group the Monkees. The movie was a bit of a mess, partly I suspect because everybody involved was whacked-out on LSD, and partly because Bob was so sick of Monkee-mania that he was purposely trying to kill it.

Wes said, "Obviously, I want you to be in it, but my question is, would you be willing to play yourself and Freddy, or are you trying to distance yourself from Freddy?"

"Wes, if you're behind it, count me in."

"Great. I'll be in touch."

I couldn't wait. But it turned out I had to.

THE FOLLOWING YEAR, I was approached to play the Marquis de Sade. When I learned that the movie—which came to be called *Night Terrors*—was going to be filmed in Alexandria, Egypt, I jumped at the chance. If I was getting paid to visit the pyramids, it didn't matter that I was playing a kinky old reprobate. An exotic stamp on my passport, a hookah, and a harem girl sounded better than singed eyebrows and an oozing face.

But then the whole project went through a radical transformation. First, for creative reasons, the script was changed, so now, instead of its being about the Marquis de Sade, it was based on a collection of the Marquis de Sade's erotic short stories and would be updated to the 1920s, and I'd be playing a decadent descendant of the marquis, as well as de Sade himself in a series of historical flashbacks that would bookend the film. Second, the film location would be transferred from Egypt to Tel Aviv, Israel. The producers were concerned that with the change of venue, I'd bail on the project, but working in any part of the Middle East sounded like an adventure to me, so I told them I was still on board. Then at the last second, another change: the filmmakers weren't able to find any 1920s prop cars in Israel, so they had to alter the script and change it from a period film to a contemporary time frame. Then the director they'd lined up—whom I had taken several meetings with and was really looking forward to working with—quit the project.

I'd already signed the contract, been paid, and had deposited the money in the bank, so I was stuck. I wasn't too thrilled about it, and the producers realized it, so to keep me happy, they hired one of my favorite directors. Guess who. Tobe Hooper. The thought of Tobe and I creating S&M mayhem on the sunny Mediterranean coast of Tel Aviv was indeed rejuvenating.

Tobe was as hands-on and as cheerful as I'd ever seen him. He would grab the camera and lie down on his back on a skateboard in the middle of the cobblestone streets of Old Jaffa and propel himself crablike, just to get the right shot. Each night after we wrapped, Tobe, his girlfriend Rita, Nancy, and I went out to dinner, usually at a waterfront restaurant, where we'd devour the catch of the day, drink a frosty pitcher of vodka-spiked lemonade, and enjoy a history lesson from Mr. Hooper. One evening as we polished off a platter of fresh calamari, Tobe pointed out a rock shelf jutting up out of the sea and said, "I think that's the legendary rock Andromeda was chained to when she was to be sacrificed to the sea monster." And he was right. Keep that in mind the next time you watch *The Texas Chain Saw Massacre;* not only can this man scare the bejesus out of you, he can also teach you a thing or two about Greek mythology.

This was 1992, a rare moment of optimism in contemporary Israel. The Oslo Accords were being negotiated, and it looked as if there might actually be lasting peace in the Middle East. Half of our crew was Arab and half was Israeli, and they worked together, shoulder to shoulder, in harmony. We went with some of our new friends from the crew to hear the rock group Simply Red perform at Sultan's Pool, the vortex of the Holy Land. Under that calm, moonlit Jerusalem sky, surrounded by that diverse young crowd, one couldn't possibly imagine the suicide bombings and random violence to come.

Wes had finally finished the script for his deconstructed *New Nightmare,* so after I'd starred in a couple of TV movies, it was finally time for me to dust off the ol' glove, get the sweater out of mothballs, suck it up, and confront that damn makeup chair again. This was going to be Wes's final farewell to Freddy, and with Wes, Heather, and John Saxon on board, it felt like a ten-year family reunion.

This was Wes's opportunity to answer his critics, reinvigorate the franchise, and return for the last time to Elm Street. It was also a chance for us to tease the fans with exaggerated depictions of our public personas. Bob Shaye and New Line executive Sara Risher also showed up to wink at the audience with self-deprecating cameos. For the veteran cast and crew, it offered us a sense of closure in a quality movie that we could all be proud of.

Freddy fanatics might be surprised to learn that *New Nightmare* is my favorite film in the series. Every time I've seen it, I've discovered something new that I'd missed before, a subtle change in Heather's wardrobe, a blurred edge between reality and the dreamscape, the savvy integration of real Los Angeles terror (e.g., earthquakes) with movie horror. The credit for all that goes to Wes. We trusted his instincts and followed his lead in this new horror hybrid. *New Nightmare* made some noise, but it wasn't boffo box office like *Nightmares* 3 and 4.

But after Wes's first *Scream* film hit movie theaters three years later, *New Nightmare* was rediscovered on DVD and has now achieved the cult status it deserves. (I believe that *New Nightmare* had laid the groundwork and contributed to the hugely successful *Scream* series. Audiences were drawn to people like themselves being depicted in these films. The characters were young, hip to pop-culture horror movies and references, and knew the ins and outs, the contrivances, of the formula horror-movie plot. Wes was the first to acknowledge this audience, and *New Nightmare* was the first film to exploit that. I was proud to have been part of this smart, scary, experimental valentine to our fans.)

Shortly after *New Nightmare* opened, Tobe Hooper called. He wanted to know if I'd be interested in going up to Toronto to star in *The Mangler*, an adaptation of an early Stephen King short story about an old-fashioned industrial laundry machine that eats people. This was a no-brainer: in all the years I'd been doing horror, I'd never done a Stephen King project, and I'll always jump at a chance to work with Tobe, so I was in.

Immediately after I signed off on the deal, I learned that Canada was out, and South Africa was in. (Notice a trend here?) No problem; another exotic entry in my passport. I'd never been to Africa and had no idea what to expect. Would there be prostitutes assigned to my room as in the Philippines? Armed teenage soldiers as in Hungary? Flammable Styrofoam sets? I was concerned because I was once again going to have to suffer through an extreme special effects makeup application and I hoped for at least a modicum of comfort. I knew by now that when working in foreign locales that standard was sometimes difficult to achieve. But when I found out that my old makeup man David Miller was on the project, my fears were alleviated.

In the ten years since the first *Nightmare*, David had kept busy, working on such diverse movies as *The Addams Family*, *Naked Gun 33⅓*, and the classic *Tremors*. For a lesser makeup man, *The Mangler* could have been viewed as a tough gig because Stephen King had only given the briefest description of my character's look, so there wasn't much to work with. For David, however, this was liberating.

None of my fans would've guessed that my main inspiration for the character came from the mind of Orson Welles and a brilliant performance by Everett Sloane. In 1947, Welles wrote, directed, and starred in a classic film noir with Rita Hayworth called *The Lady from Shanghai*, in which one of the supporting players had polio and was forced to wear cumbersome leg braces and walk with dual arm-fitted crutches.

I borrowed those elements, then added a dash of Harry Truman's can-do personality, and, presto, I'd fleshed out Stephen King's quick character sketch. I'd solved the look and mannerisms of King's lecherous Bill Gartley, who remains one of the vilest, most cantankerous SOBs on my résumé. If you are gonna steal, steal from the best.

Just as on my first day on the Hollywood set of Tobe Hooper's *Eaten Alive* back in 1977, I was knocked on my ass when I walked on the soundstage in Johannesburg and saw what had been built there. That seemingly interminable flight from L.A. to Joburg was instantly forgiven. Most impressive was the hulking Hadley-Watson Mangler itself, created by Tobe's son, Tony. It was the laundry folder from hell, the scariest death-machine I've ever worked with. (The fucking thing actually worked—if you got too close to it, you were toast.) The set was formidable, with its crisscrossing catwalks, three-story industrial staircases, and a system of aerial conveyor belts constantly circulating soiled canvas laundry bags like spider's prey cocooned in a web. It was like some hellish factory from a Kafka novel. I marveled at this dark, atmospheric tableau and once again knew I'd made the right decision to schlep halfway around the world to work with such an imaginative, visionary director as Tobe Hooper.

David Miller's original makeup creation was on par with the production design and I was introduced for the first time to stippling. Simply put, David stretched sections of my facial skin, then dabbed some FX secret sauce on it, blasted me with a blow-dryer, and then released my skin, which gave my face a finely creased crepe-paper look that appeared naturally old. He then applied a premade prosthetic nose, brow, a wattled turkey neck, and ears, then blended these pieces seamlessly into the previously stippled, aged skin. The Gartley makeup took as long to apply as the Freddy face because we also needed time to attach the wig of snow-white hair and blend the netted edge into the makeup. It sounds like a drag, but after seven *Nightmare* flicks, the Freddy TV series, and literally hundreds of applications, there was no makeup session I couldn't endure, even in the heat of Africa.

CHAPTER 12

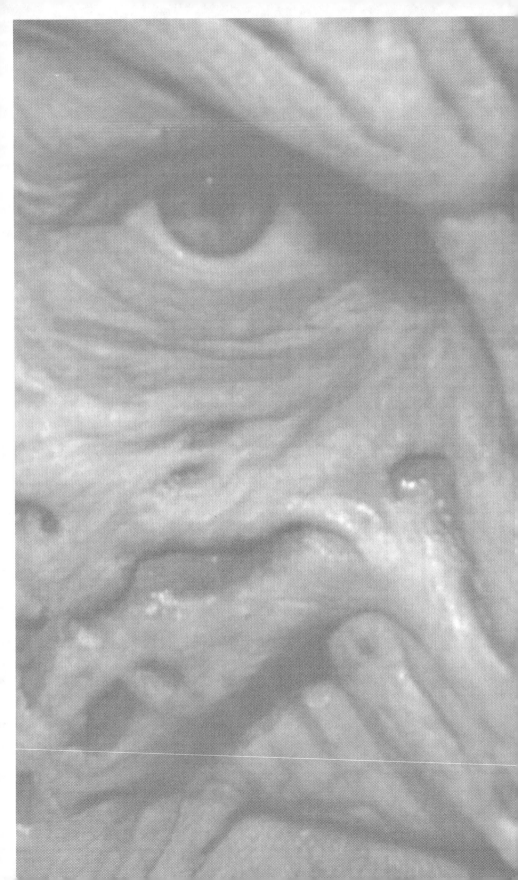

NIGHTMARE #12:

In the midst of an epic childhood reenactment of the Peter Pan versus the pirates sword fight, I was cornered against the galvanized stair treads of a heavy, stainless-steel slide. I backed my way up the stairs, and then, trapped at the top by pirates below, I threw my wooden sword in the air in surrender. Unfortunately, on its way down, it hit my best friend squarely on the top of his head. Head wounds bleed like a bitch, and upon seeing the gusher, I was as traumatized as my pal. Twelve hours later came the nightmare, in which I dueled with my friend in the sickly green hallway outside his hospital room. As blood dripped out of his scalp, he stabbed me with his blunt toy sword. Payback's a bitch.

*I*N A MEMORABLE SCENE IN THE 1982 MOVIE *Diner*, Kevin Bacon, Mickey Rourke, Steve Guttenberg, and Daniel Stern are sitting around late at night at *the* diner, arguing about the TV show *Bonanza*, and which Cartwright brother would win in a fight. That may sound silly, but on the street, at film festivals, or at virtually every sci-fi/horror/fantasy convention or Comic-Con I've appeared at, I'm asked, "Do you think Freddy could take Michael 'Halloween' Myers in a fight? Since Dracula sleeps all day, could Freddy get inside his dreams and kill him?" (Uh, does Dracula even dream?) "Mr. Englund, what do you think would happen if Freddy fought Jason from *Friday the Thirteenth*? Who'd win?" Legitimate questions all, and I guess they could keep you up at night if you're fourteen years old.

Matt Groening and his pals at *The Simpsons* were the first to pit Freddy Krueger and Jason Voorhees against one another. I was invited to voice Freddy for their 1998 Halloween special, and as *The Simpsons* is one of contemporary pop culture's touchstones, of course I was thrilled to offer my vocal talents. One of three segments on the show, it ran only about eight minutes, but it inspired somebody at New Line: *Hey, what if we get the two most successful movie monsters of the last quarter century to duke it out?*

For me, *Freddy vs. Jason* had been a long time coming. New Line and my agent went into discussions before the film even started preproduction; numerous writers tried to solve the plot logistics and find a justification for the megamonsters to meet. I don't know how long the final script had been floating around—after ten years I didn't have enough juice for script approval, and nobody was sending me copies of the endless rewrites—but it started to look as though it might be *Freddy 2000,* so I cleared my schedule.

New Line was having trouble deciding on a director, so the project was pushed to 2001, and *again* I cleared my schedule. Then it went through still more script revisions, got pushed to 2002, and this time I *didn't* bother to clear my schedule. This movie had been rumored for years, and by now the fans were getting restless, posting on chat boards questions like "Is this Freddy/Jason showdown ever going to fucking happen, or what?" Finally New Line Cinema got all their ducks in a row, and I prepared to commit to *Freddy vs. Jason.* While they were fiddling around, I'd kept busy filming half a dozen movies, both in the States and overseas, one right after the other. I wasn't as damaged as I had been going into *Nightmare 5,* but a decade had passed, and this old dog needed to do some sit-ups if he was going to duke it out in the boiler room with the goalie from hell.

For the director, our esteemed producers chose Ronny Yu, a veteran kung fu producer/director from China who, in 1998, made his first splash in the United States with *Bride of Chucky.* (I had actually presented an award to Ronny for *Chucky* with John Landis, when we both served on the jury at a boutique film festival in the French Alps.) The writing team that delivered a script everybody agreed upon, Damian Shannon and Mark Swift, were pretty green, so new that their take on the confrontation between the two horror icons was actually their first script that had gone into production. They launched their career in high style, concocting a twisted, violent mix echoing the grand tradition of *Frankenstein Meets the Wolf Man.*

We shot in Vancouver, and for the first time a *Nightmare* movie had a real, honest-to-goodness budget. Let me rephrase that: we had an honest-to-goodness BUDGET. We're talking a cool twenty-five mil, which would buy us a shitload of peanut butter. And foam latex. And glue.

I went up to Canada before any of the other actors; I had to sit through at least half a dozen makeup tests because there were going to be two versions of Freddy: "traditional" Freddy and "demonic" Freddy. (Some bloggers with no life argued that it was a Coca-Cola Classic versus New Coke situation, and we should have left well enough alone. Me, I have no problem reinventing shit.) None of the previous *Nightmare* makeup-effects people were on the new project, so we had to start from scratch.

Fortunately, our new makeup man Bill Terezakis had *game.*

A Canadian native and FX veteran of more than sixty movies, Bill has a wonderful makeup shop in the Soho-like section of Vancouver, right next door to the best Italian restaurant in the city. He had a gifted crew working for him, so I had no problem surrendering what remained of my delicate complexion to him.

Ronny Yu blew into town soon thereafter, and the two of us hit it off right away. We communicated well, and his detailed storyboards illuminated his vision and clued me in to where I fit in his frame. For a guy whose first language was Cantonese, he expressed his directorial viewpoints and goals better than half of the TV guest directors I'd worked with. Ronny was a keeper.

A COUPLE DAYS BEFORE we began filming, I was going to be introduced to the cast: first-time leading man Jason Ritter, the late, great John Ritter's son; Kelly Rowland, Beyoncé Knowles's right-hand woman in Destiny's Child; and Monica Keena, who'd costarred in an underappreciated Judd Apatow TV series *Undeclared* and went on to portray the heartbreaking ex-love of Kevin Connolly on *Entourage*. For the meeting, one of our producers had picked me up at the hotel and driven me to the suburbs. When the driver said, "We're here, Mr. Englund," I got out of the car and was astounded to find that I was at 1428 Elm Street. This house in the middle of suburban Vancouver looked exactly like Nancy Thompson's original *Nightmare* house in Springwood, Anywhere USA.

I stared at the place and said, "Jesus Christ. The art department sure did a great job on this place."

My producer said, "Not really."

"What do you mean?"

"One of the location scouts found it. They didn't have to change it at all."

My big question was, was this a coincidence, or had some

obsessed *Nightmare* freak actually replicated the Elm Street house? Regardless of the answer, the house was perfect and a good omen for a good shoot. (The original *Nightmare* house just south of Sunset bordering West Hollywood has recently been lovingly restored to its vintage Elm Street splendor. Don't tell 'em I sent ya.)

In the previous *Nightmare* films, my mission was to stalk and kill beautiful teenage girls, hang out in various Elm Street bedrooms, and get set on fire over and over again. That all required a fair amount of physical exertion certainly, but nothing that could be considered out of the ordinary for a horror-film heavy. There was the occasional stunt—including those motherfucking fire gags—and the inevitable, unending makeup sessions, but all in all, those shoots were painless.

On *Freddy vs. Jason*, however, Ronny Yu brought the pain. As an active surfer and bodyboarder, I was still in pretty decent shape, but I wasn't a kid anymore—I was in my mid-fifties when Ronny first called "Action"—and didn't expect that I'd be run ragged. Jesus, Mary, and Joseph, was I wrong. Doing a single stunt-take wasn't that much of a problem for me, but after repeating it from several different angles, my fiftysomething-year-old bones began to complain. But I refused to pussy out and went about my stunt work without whining. Okay, without *too* much whining, but that's still pretty good for an old dog.

I'd planned to avoid fire stunts at all costs, but, since I was comfortable in the ocean, I volunteered to do my own water stunts, some of which involved being submerged in Jason's Crystal Lake. Bill Terezakis and his team were nervous about what would happen with the makeup when I was underwater—they didn't give a damn if I drowned, so long as their prosthetics survived intact—so when they pieced together the Freddy makeup for the underwater shoot, they lathered extra glue on my face. (Remember that this medical adhesive was originally designed for use on colostomy bags. This confirms the belief of some *Nightmare* critics that I was a real shithead.) Once everybody was happy with the look, into the water I went.

The stunts went off without a hitch, and, waterlogged, I slogged back to the makeup trailer, eager to get all the glue off my face. Bill's aide-de-camp Patricia Murray went to work on me, then, after a minute, she said, "Ummm . . . Robert?"

"Yeah?"

"We have a problem."

This conversation felt awfully familiar. "What kind of problem?"

"The kind of problem where some of this shit is stuck." Talk about déjà vu. It was *Nightmare 2* all over again.

"How did that happen?"

"My guess is that between the water and the chlorine and the extra glue, we got screwed."

"You mean *I* got screwed."

"Semantics."

"So what now?" I asked.

"I scrub."

And scrub she did. Patricia buffed my face as gently as she could with a sponge that could be used to remove burnt oatmeal from the bottom of a pot. I wasn't freaking out because I knew she'd get it off eventually, but we'd just finished a fourteen-hour day, and as is always the case when I'm in full makeup, I didn't eat much of anything. I was starving, and more importantly, I craved a cocktail, but unless I wanted to hit the hotel bar looking like a waterlogged demon, I'd have to suffer.

Finally, two hours later, I was free of the last of the latex, but my skin was a disaster, especially my eyes, which were so swollen that it looked as if I'd gone ten rounds with Mike Tyson. Or maybe Jason Voorhees. (P.S. The next day, I pleaded with Patricia to go easy on the glue. She said she'd try her best, but she couldn't use too little because she had to make certain that no water would seep up inside the Freddy makeup from the area where it adhered to my clavicle. If it did, she said, I'd fill up and look like a giant, used condom.)

Jason was played by Canadian stunt coordinator/stuntman Ken Kirzinger. Ken, who's about six feet five inches and weighs a biscuit short of 275, had worked in one capacity or another on approximately one hundred films, including *X/2*, *X-Men: The Last Stand*, and *The Incredible Hulk*, and TV shows such as *X-Files* and *Smallville*, but here he was making what might be called his acting debut. (Ken, who was initially interviewing to be our stunt coordinator, was offered the part the second Ronny laid eyes on him. "I want Jason to be larger than life," he told Ken, "and you're my Jason.") Ken and I became fast friends and drinking buddies, which is fortunate, because as an average-size guy who was going to have to film lengthy fight scenes with a giant, I needed to trust he wouldn't squash me like a bug.

Our first night shoot of the Freddy/Jason showdown at the lake was also the first day of fall, and right on cue the temperature plummeted from the upper sixties to the middle forties, not ideal conditions for splashing around in a Canadian lake for a week. From the moment we started, it was surreal: we set the lake on fire, with Navy SEALS in arctic-issue wet suits on the scene in case one of us needed some help, and we were all freezing our collective asses off. Ken, Jason, Monica, and I kept hypothermia away by jumping into a bubbling hot tub after every take, immediately after Ronny yelled, "Cut!" Looking back, I'm not sure if it was the cold or Monica in her skimpy, wet wardrobe that kept the boys constantly hot-tubbing.

Several nights into shooting at the lake, Patricia was applying the Freddy makeup one evening when all of a sudden we heard a loud *BOOM*. After the trailer stopped shaking, we ran outside, and there, right in the middle of this beautiful body of water, twenty minutes from civilization, there's a fuckin' mini–mushroom cloud. It wasn't Hiroshima by any means, but it was shocking nonetheless. Turned out that thanks to our setting the lake on fire three nights in a row, a gasoline slick had gotten trapped under our fake pier. One of the Teamsters was smoking a cigarette, then tossed the butt in the lake and almost blew up half of British Columbia—which didn't exactly give me confidence as I headed into yet another fire sequence.

Yes, that's right, I got talked into a fire stunt again. For one of our battles, Ken and I had to tussle in a small room with flame bars attached to all four walls. (Flame bars are exactly what you think they'd be: gas-fed pipes that you can light on fire on cue.) They shot the scene from Ken's perspective first, which meant the fire was directly behind me, and that sucker was hot. Ronny—who was, it seemed, getting more sadistic by the minute—asked for take, after take, after take; he wanted to get every angle imaginable, in front of me, behind me, bird's-eye view, between my legs. Between the flame bars, the fight action, my head encased in foam, and that goddamned striped sweater, I thought I was going to die in that tiny, overheated room.

Finally they turned the cameras around, and it was Ken's turn to enjoy dancing with flame bars. First take, the flame bar is lit, and he saunters at me with his cool, slow Jason walk, menacingly wielding his machete, and it was perfect. Second take, fine. Third take, ditto. Unlike yours truly when I had my ass to the flames, Ken was actually enjoying his John Wayne moment and was happy to try it again and again. On take four, Ken raised his machete even more deliberately than on the previous three, and as the fire behind him crept higher and higher, Ken walked toward me menacingly, unaware that the set wall behind him was completely engulfed in flames, when all of a sudden his extended machete-wielding arm started smoking. Then his shoulder. Then his hockey mask started to steam. I'm there yelling, "Come on, Jason! Come to Papa," while my nemesis is about to burst into flames.

He was seconds away from full dorsal incineration when I broke character and said, "Excuse me, kind sir, but it appears that your costume has suffered a bit of smoke damage, and I think it would be wise of you to vacate the premises. Immediately." Or something to that effect. As was the case with the gas bomb at the lake, nobody was hurt. Much.

SINCE VANCOUVER CAN BE made up to look more or less like any city or suburb in the United States, a surprising percentage of Hollywood films are filmed north of the border.

There are only so many nice hotels in the area, so most productions shooting there house their respective casts and crews at the same places. We shared a hotel with the gang that was shooting the second installment of the *X-Men* series, and on the way to work I'd take the elevator down to the lobby with the likes of Patrick Stewart and Hugh Jackman, which is every fanboy's dream. Their shoot seemed never-ending, and aside from Patrick Stewart, who always seem to be in a good mood, practically everybody on the production was going a little crazy. (Apparently Alan Cumming was more irked than anybody else, especially when he was in FX makeup all damn day and never even got on film. Welcome to *my* world, Nightcrawler.)

We showbiz types hadn't commandeered every room in the hotel; there were also a bunch of elderly Englishwomen who'd flown across the pond to enjoy Vancouver Island's famous gardens. One morning, I got off the elevator and was greeted by the sight of Hugh Jackman besieged by half a dozen little old ladies. I thought, *What the fuck is this about? They can't be Wolverine fans.*

On the way out to wait for my car, I asked the concierge, "What's going on here? Why's Hugh such a hit with the grannies?"

He said, "They all saw him do *Oklahoma* in London a few years back. He played Curly." Then the concierge began humming "Oh What a Beautiful Mornin'."

I said, "Thanks for the serenade," then I waited for my driver to take me to the set. He was running late, so I hung in the lobby for fifteen minutes, and the entire time Hugh signed and chatted, kissed hands, and posed for photos. I'd like to point out that not a single one of these women asked me for my autograph. I guess the *Oklahoma* demographic and the *Nightmare* demographic didn't have much crossover.

Freddy vs. Jason opened in August of 2003, and it brought in $36 million on its first weekend, well eclipsing the $25 million budget. It ended up taking in over $86 million U.S. theatrical alone and was the most lucrative film I had ever been associated with, a legitimate blockbuster, and I decided that that was it for me and Freddy. It was the right time to move on.

I assume *Freddy vs. Jason* attracted such a wide audience because *A Nightmare on Elm Street* has transcended generations; some of the fans who had seen the first *Nightmare* back in 1984 were now parents, many of whom were eager to introduce Freddy Krueger and the fond memory of their *Nightmare on Elm Street* thrills to their jaded kids.

Because, as Freddy Krueger might say, the family that plays together, slays together.

EPILOGUE

BEYOND THE NIGHTMARES

*I*T'S BEEN SAID THAT IF A SHARK STOPS moving, it will die. Well, I've gotta work or I'm dead in the water. And I'm not talking about some surfing accident. I don't care whether a movie of mine makes $1 or $1 billion; I'll probably be in front of or behind the camera until the final "Cut" is called.

One of the most enjoyable aspects of being a working character actor is that, in addition to the luminaries previously mentioned in this tome, over the years on both the big screen and the small screen, I've had the opportunity and privilege to hit my marks with some of the best in the business, among them Hal Holbrook, James Earl Jones, Sissy Spacek, Lou Gossett, Brian Cox, Pat Hingle, and Jack Warden.

I appeared on two of the more popular sitcoms of the late '90s: *Married . . . With Children,* and *The Jamie Foxx Show*—two lovely experiences. (On our lunch break, I overheard Jamie playing Gershwin on the piano on an empty soundstage. Magical.) And along with Stephen Colbert, Margaret Cho, Janeane Garofalo, Fred Willard, Virginia Madsen, Mike Myers, and practically everyone else in Hollywood, including an uncredited Ben Stiller, I appeared in a nasty little showbiz parody called *Nobody Knows Anything,* which—in yet another Six-Degrees-of-Kevin-Bacon kind of coincidence—starred my *Hollywood Monster* co-writer Alan Goldsher's pal, David Pasquesi.

Hell, I even dabbled in reality television. Screw *Survivor.* Fuck *Big Brother.* I had *Reel Nightmares.*

In 2004, an award-winning director/producer/writer/jack-of-all-television named Star Price came up with another winning idea: send the guy who played Freddy Krueger all over the country to interview people about their scariest, sickest nightmares, then set up a soundstage in L.A., turn their dreams into a frightening reality, and haul their asses out to Hollywood to live through their nightmares on camera. *This was reality* television, baby. Star, who went on to produce and direct most every episode of *Penn & Teller: Bullshit!,* clearly had his finger on the pulse of the new media phenomenon (knew his shit), and I wanted in.

Reel Nightmares had what I considered a distinctive format. In the beginning of each episode, I'd visit our victim's neighborhood, taking a shortcut through a dark alley or over a backyard fence, then I'd approach the front door and knock. In my best Vincent Price inflection, I would announce: "Hello. My name is Robert Englund, and I understand there's a nightmare on your street." We'd then cut to me sitting in their living room and grilling them about their most demented dreams. While they recounted these very personal nightmares, I'd ask them all sorts of probing psychological questions that made everybody uncomfortable, myself included. After we watched the footage, we took the best-of-the-best subjects and sent them to speak with our legal department, to make sure they weren't litigious or nuts or completely full of shit. Then, once they jumped through all the legal and ethical hoops, it was off to California, where they'd get to find out just how much fun it is to be on Elm Street. The best part is that we had a nice budget, and while you can scare the crap out of somebody with a small budget, it's certainly easier to make somebody puke or poop or pee their pants when your pockets are deep.

Despite that Star, our intrepid *Reel Nightmares* skeleton crew, and I gave it our all—we're talking back-to-back cross-country flights from Chicago to Los Angeles, cheap fleet puddle jumpers from Atlanta to Little Rock, combined with multiple all-nighters—we never made it on the air. If I were casting blame—and I'm not, mind you—but if I were, I'd have to point my finger at *Fear Factor*. Mind you, I have no animosity toward Joe Rogan. It's just that his show's success kind of fucked us.

In both television and film, networks and studios tend to stick with a concept or a format that's already proven to be a winner. For instance, for the three years after *Friends* became a hit, I would estimate that three out of every five new sitcoms featured an ensemble of twentysomethings trying to find themselves in the big city. The reasoning behind that is obvious—every new product is a gamble, and producers want to stack the decks in their favor—but that sometimes means that a more original project gets shelved.

It shouldn't have surprised anybody on the *Reel Nightmares* team that most of the networks' notes encouraged us to focus on finding people whose dreams were about being scared of snakes or bugs, or eating monkey brains. Thing is, chilling in a snake-filled bathtub and chowing down on a goat-bladder soufflé had already been done, so the shock value and the sense of newness were gone. To us, *Fear Factor* gross was already passé. The networks' attitudes pissed Star and me off because when we veered away from the *Fear Factor* vibe, we found we had something original and special.

One of our strongest segments featured a young lady who was petrified of clowns, which apparently, a surprising number of people can relate to. (Me, I'm not scared of clowns at all. Fuck them. I can kick a clown's ass any day of the week. Okay, that's sheer bravado. The fact of the matter is, if you want to give me a mild freak-out, stick me in an elevator with Bozo.) We took this poor girl and locked her in a turn-of-the-century Victorian mansion near downtown Los Angeles, where she was hunted by a posse of psycho clowns—think Cirque de Soleil channeled through the Jim Rose Circus—all decked out in the scariest, smeared, avant-garde makeup you've seen this side of, well, Freddy Krueger.

We hid those killer clowns all over the house in some pretty strange positions, the two freakiest being the one who was submerged in a blood-filled bathtub, and the one inside a jerry-rigged medicine cabinet, waiting to lunge when she came looking for sleeping pills. Gotcha! Hidden cameras were *everywhere*: in the ceiling, beneath the floorboards, behind mirrors—clown-cams were even attached to some of the tormentors. None of this was a surprise for our subject; we followed her blueprint, and she knew what was coming. But then she had to experience our reconstruction of her deepest fears. When I saw the raw footage, it was intense stuff. Suffice it to say, I was glad I wasn't in her clown shoes.

Yes, the *Fear Factor* paradigm cost us, but what killed us in the end was the legal red tape. Most of our subjects didn't pass the psychological vetting; I'm not sure what criteria they used, but if our lawyers saw even the slightest hint of a red flag, they put the kibosh on the contestant, protecting our backs in the event of a lawsuit or a nervous breakdown . . . or suicide by clown. We pushed the envelope too hard, so unfortunately *Reel Nightmares* never saw the light of day. It was disappointing because we had all worked so hard and were so close to getting the show just right.

WORKING ON *REEL NIGHTMARES* took up most of 2004, which meant that I had to turn down a number of other projects, projects I might not have been offered had *Freddy vs. Jason* not turned into such a megahit. I had to pass on one job that was shooting in Italy, and another that was set near a resort in Mexico. I don't recall if the scripts were any good, but after a year of shuttling around feeder city airports chasing down damaged dreamers, the thought of taking a vacation while I was working was pretty damn appealing.

After a couple weeks of R&R, I started plowing through the pile of screenplays that had been building by my bedside. A number of them were quite good, and, me being me, I said yes to those I liked. I starred with Bob Shaye's sister Lin in a funky retro slasher flick *2001 Maniacs*, written and directed by an old acquaintance, Tim Sullivan. (Fans of *There's Something About Mary* will remember Lin as Cameron Diaz's obnoxious dog-owning, saggy-titted neighbor.) I'd known Tim since his days as an assistant to Michael DeLuca at New Line. Tim had been associate producer on a little gem of a film, *Detroit Rock City*, which starred one of my favorite underground actors, Giuseppe Andrews. Tim wrote and tailored the role of Mayor Buckman for my peculiar talents and promised me I'd get to work with Giuseppe. How could I say no? There was plenty of blood and gore, tits and ass, and Vaudeville-style violence—Tim and I often refer to that sort of collision of styles as "splatstick."

In 2005, I again reunited with good ol' Tobe Hooper for an episode of Showtime's *Masters of Horror* series called *Dance of the Dead*. We shot it up in Vancouver, on the set of Jessica Alba's TV show *Dark Angel*. In *Dance of the Dead*, an adaptation of a Richard Matheson short story, I played a postapocalyptic emcee at a nightclub where we inject dead strippers with a serum that reanimates them and they commence a spastic death-dance, hence the title. Tobe had a great budget to work with and went all out, and to this day I feel it's one of the edgiest hours of television produced for cable. It's Peckinpah-violent, decadent, kinky, and driven by a percussive, post-punk soundtrack.

Almost immediately after we wrapped, I was once again out in the hot Santa Clarita boondocks to cameo in *Hatchet*. This time out I played—are you ready for this?—a victim! I met my fate in a backlot swamp and my killer was none other than Kane Hodder, everybody's favorite Jason Voorhees. Kane portrayed Victor Crowley, a deformed madman, and was under more makeup than I'd ever had to wear, plus a prosthetic hunchback. I felt his pain.

And then came a Sam-Loomis-meets-Van-Helsing turn in *Behind the Mask: The Rise of Leslie Vernon*, a distinctly *Blair Witch*-y flick that won critical praise. Then it was up to Toronto for *Heartstopper*, where I played a small-town sheriff and got my ass kicked by a serial killer. Again in Canada, this time Ottawa, I shot the horror comedy *Jack Brooks: Monster*

Slayer, in which I played a community college science teacher who gets possessed by a cursed, black heart. And then in 2008, I costarred with Jenna Jameson in *Zombie Strippers!* (yes, there was an exclamation mark in the title), wishing the whole time that I'd been given the opportunity when I was fourteen. Victims? Doctors? Sheriffs? Professors? Hanging out with porn stars? Man, you take off the makeup, and next thing you know, they're casting you as professional types who contribute to society. Yikes.

These assorted retro-horror projects didn't garner *Nightmare* numbers at the box office, but they all found loyal, appreciative audiences, I think in part as a reaction to the big, overproduced special effects extravaganzas that relied too much on all of Hollywood's new toys and gadgets. Don't get me wrong: toys and gadgets can be a blast, but instead of inspiring writers and directors to greater heights, the new technology tends to make people ignore script, story, and plot problems. Too often you'll hear on the set of a blockbuster-in-the-making that's running five weeks behind schedule and $5 million over budget, "We'll fix it in post." FX should be used as enhancement, not as a Band-Aid for something you overlooked during pre-production or screwed up during principal photography.

Audiences know when you are relying on explosions and CGI because your story sucks or your scares aren't there. And I think their frustration led to a nostalgia for good old blood 'n' guts and cheap thrills. Fortunately, a generation of young filmmakers—Eli Roth, Adam Green, Scott Glosserman, Tim Sullivan, to name a few—understand this and look to Tobe Hooper and John Carpenter for inspiration, rather than their

Mac Pro. If you want to put it in a musical context, it reminds me of the late 1970s, when rock fans got fed up with balding supergroups and prog-rock jerk-offs, instead choosing to embrace loud minimalist punkers such as MC5, Iggy Pop, the Ramones, and the New York Dolls. Iggy et al. were alternatives to the bloat in the music industry, and breathed a new life into the art form by reexamining the root source of rock 'n' roll. Splatstick, retro-slasher, and torture porn were embracing the roots of horror and had discovered an audience, and I understood why. It was the garage rock of horror. The fact that Sam Raimi's *Evil Dead* franchise and Wes's *Scream* trio had set the table for the horror/comedy mash-up didn't hurt either.

All the retro-oriented work brought me back to the beginning of my horror career, but it was actually several years *prior* when everything really came full circle.

IN 1999, I WAS invited to the Rome Fanta Film Festival, where I was honored with a retrospective of my work. While there, I met the directing team of Daniele Cipri and Franco Maresco, who invited me to Sicily to speak to an audience of teens from housing projects on the outskirts of Palermo. Why would these gentlemen want to use the actor who plays Freddy Krueger to talk movies with these kids? Turns out that Cipri and Maresco had built an audience-friendly boutique cinema right there in the middle of what could be termed a suburban wasteland. I suspect their thinking was along the lines of, *These kids all know who Freddy Krueger is, and perhaps Robert can inspire them to appreciate quality movies and perhaps motivate them to pursue film careers. Plus it'll keep them off the streets.*

When I walked into their theater, the first thing I saw in the lobby was an Italian poster of my 1978 surfer movie, *Big Wednesday*, retitled *Un Mercoledì da Leoni*. Right next to that was a poster for one of my favorite horror films in history, Brian De Palma's *Sisters*. Cipri, Maresco, and I were most definitely on the same wavelength, so I wasn't at all surprised when the following year they asked me to be the first American to star in one of their films.

In the spring and summer of both 2001 and 2002, I went to Sicily, where Cipri and Maresco directed me in a black comedy called *The Return of Cagliostro*, or, for you Italian linguists out there, *Il Ritorno di Cagliostro*. The Cagliostro of the title was Alessandro Cagliostro, a real-life Italian huckster who lived in the eighteenth century. Cagliostro claimed to be the son of the prince and princess of the Anatolian Christian kingdom of Trebizond, but in reality, good ol' Al was born into poverty and bullshitted his way through life as an alchemist, magician, and con man, gaining fame when he became involved in a diamond scam with Marie Antoinette. Good ol' Al intrigued many a film producer, and he's been depicted by Orson Welles (*Black Magic* in 1949), and Christopher Walken (*The Affair of the Necklace* in 2001), and Robert Englund. Well, *sort of* by Robert Englund.

In Cipri and Maresco's take on the Cagliostro story, I was playing an over-the-hill American actor who was conned into going to Italy by Lucky Luciano to play good ol' Al in a bogus movie that existed strictly to launder mob money through the Catholic church. (To represent my character's Hollywood pedigree, he was named Erroll Douglas. That's "Erroll" as in "Flynn," and "Douglas" as in "Kirk.") The movie within the movie is purposely horrible, so the high-concept, one-sentence pitch for the project might've been, "It's *The Producers* meets *Bugsy* set in Italy in the 1950s." I'd pay my ten bucks to see something like that.

Since it happened over two summers, in a sense this was the longest film shoot I'd ever been a part of, but that wasn't because Cipri and Maresco, darlings of the Left and committed auteurs who many consider to be Italy's answer to the Coen brothers, were perfectionists. What slowed them down was that they insisted on peppering the cast with non-actors. Not novice actors. Not bad actors. Non-actors! Some of them couldn't quite remember their lines or hit their marks or do a scene the same way twice. On the other hand, several were comic originals, and had developed a cult following in Italy, so Cipri and Maresco were perfectly content with their eccentricities. I wasn't sure where I fit into all of this, but, trouper that I am, I put on my metaphorical crash helmet, strapped in, and went along for the ride.

Early on, we were shooting a scene in a subterranean wine cellar at an old villa on the coast outside Palermo. The cellar set was lit entirely by the torches mounted on the wall and held by the other actors and extras in the scene. (Cipri and Maresco loved the quality of light provided by the smoky torches.) My character was supposed to throw a tantrum in the scene, which prompted me to pitch a diva fit of my own; however, mine was completely justified.

After a few takes, we all started getting lethargic because the fire was sucking the oxygen out of the room, and I thought, *Shit, this is* A Nightmare on Elm Street *all over again.* One of the non-actors got so oxygen-deprived that he slid down the wall and onto the floor. As he nodded off, his torch slowly tipped over and it almost ignited the hem of one of the "priest's" cassock costumes.

I snapped. I lost it. "What the hell are you doing?" I roared. "There are no fire extinguishers on the set and the cellar door is fucking closed!" I stormed over to the ancient doors and threw them open. After about five more minutes of ranting and raving, I clammed up; and fortunately, no animals or humans were harmed in the making of *The Return of Cagliostro.*

The film safety notwithstanding, this region of Italy was a magnificent place to shoot, utterly timeless, with acres of rolling hills and ancient vineyards, crumbling villas, and ruins. We were so far removed from civilization that sometimes the only sound to be heard was the cooing of pigeons, or the clockwork tolling of church bells.

For a while, my dressing room was in the basement of a monastery. On the plaster wall, somebody had written PRE-GATE! PREGATE! PREGATE! in blood. (*Pregate* means "pray.") By the time the second summer of shooting rolled around, I was so sick of the tights that Erroll Douglas wore for the sham Cagliostro movie-within-a-movie that I was *pregate*-ing for a wardrobe change.

One afternoon, there was a tentative knock at my dressing-room door. I opened it, and there stood the cutest little Italian punk-rock girl on that historic island. She had a delicate ring in her nose and fine, gold thread laced up her earlobe, a map of tattoos, and black bangs that contrasted beautifully with her porcelain skin. My first thought was, *What's she doing in a monastery?* Then she brought in some crisp white linens, some mismatched fine china, a soup terrine, and what appeared to be the family silver. Turned out she was the set caterer, and what a caterer she was. There, in the middle of the Sicilian countryside, I was served one of the finest meals I'd ever had, five perfect courses that would probably have cost about three bills in Manhattan. The coup de grâce was a limoncello that her grandfather had decanted that morning. Craft service in the States was never like this.

On my second-to-last morning shooting in Palermo, I woke up and my legs were covered with blood. The white sheets on my hotel bed were a disaster, so bloody that I thought there might be a decapitated horse head under the blankets. I jumped out of bed, and noticed my thighs were covered with scratches. My first thought: *bedbugs.* Nope. Not even close. Turned out that those tights I'd been wearing—which had been on loan from an old opera company—were infested with lice. It was time to go home.

But it was all worth it. *Cagliostro* was released in 2003, shortly before *Freddy vs. Jason* opened worldwide, and that fall, Cipri, Maresco, our producers, and I were invited to the Venice Film Festival for the premiere of our film.

Full house.

The lights went down.

The projector fired up.

The film played.

The credits rolled.

The lights went up.

The crowd rose as one, and we got a ten-minute standing ovation.

They wouldn't stop. Seriously, they wouldn't fucking stop. It went on, and on, and on, and finally I accepted it. I got a lump in my throat, my face went hot, and tears spilled onto my cheeks. It was one of the greatest moments in my life, and feeling all that respect from my fellow film lovers, I wondered, to quote David Byrne, *Well, how did I get here?*

The route, as circuitous as it was, was beautiful in its symmetry. A showbiz-adjacent California boy . . . a kid fascinated with Lon Chaney . . . children's theater star . . . a teenage surfer . . . twentysomething Anglophile stage snob . . . 70s indie-film chameleon . . . television alien lizard . . . international iconic bogeyman . . . and finally, post-millennium indie-film character actor once again. Along with the masks of comedy and tragedy, I'd worn the mask of Freddy Krueger close to twenty years and I was finally comfortable to retire it.

AFTERWORD

And now a few Where Are They Nows:

WES CRAVEN

Since we worked together on *New Nightmare*, Wes's career has gone to the next level. He's written, produced, or executive-produced almost thirty films and has practically become a brand name. In terms of creativity, popularity, and critical reception, *Scream 1*, *Scream 2*, and *Scream 3* have to be regarded as his greatest successes, but I think he'll always have a special place in his heart for Mr. Krueger.

BOB SHAYE

Bob has done nothing since Freddy hung up his claw—that is, if you consider executive-producing all three *Lord of the Rings* movies nothing. The first movie he executive-produced was John Waters's *Polyester*, which had a budget of $300,000. For *The Lord of the Rings: The Two Towers*, we're talking ninety-four mil. Something tells me that the next time I work with Bob Shaye, there won't be any peanut-butter sandwiches on the set.

AFTERWORD

KEVIN YAGHER

This guy takes on so many makeup and FX gigs that I have no idea how he fits in time for food, sleep, or sex. We're talking TV series such as *Bones,* sci-fi flicks such as *Matrix II* and *III,* dramas such as *Adaptation,* and comedies such as *Anger Management*—not to mention that he owns his own company, Kevin Yagher Productions. Unfortunately, what with all this movie work, he hasn't had a chance to hone his stand-up act and hit the comedy clubs.

TOBE HOOPER

Tobe is selective about his projects and only takes on gigs he feels are worthy of his time and energy. (Not exactly working-stiff behavior, wouldn't you say?) *The Texas Chain Saw Massacre* remains the defining moment of his wonderful career, and I'm certain that he was pleased with the 2003 remake starring the hot Jessica Biel. As of this writing, he's announced plans to pen an original horror novel with the expert assistance of one Alan Goldsher, and is getting ready to direct an adaptation of another Stephen King work, *From a Buick 8.* Considering his excellent work on *The Mangler,* I have high hopes.

HEATHER LANGENKAMP

Aside from being an exemplary mother, Heather has taken baby steps behind-the-scenes, most notably when she worked on the Steve Carell comedy *Evan Almighty* as a special effects makeup coordinator. I find the thought of her imprisoning some poor sap in a makeup chair hugely ironic and completely hilarious.

JOHNNY DEPP

The artist once known as Oprah Noodlemantra is one of the busiest men on the planet. He's either off doing another *Pirates of the Caribbean* flick or appearing in a trippy movie such as *Charlie and the Chocolate Factory* or *Sweeney Todd,* or starring in and executive-producing a personal project such as Hunter S. Thompson's *The Rum Diary,* or he's flying to France to be with his girlfriend, Vanessa Paradis, and their two children. Hopefully he's learned to chuck his Christmas trees when they go bad.

GARY BUSEY

Gary has become his own man, an individualist who does what he wants, says what he wants, and ingests what he wants. His reputation has taken a beating—sometimes justifiably so—so folks tend to forget that back in the day, Gary had the potential to become one of the leading acting lights of his generation. He has a ton of talent, and I hope that he can rise from the ashes and show us the kind of chops he demonstrated back in 1978, when he landed an Oscar nomination for *The Buddy Holly Story.* (That said, if he ever invites me out for lunch, I'm bringing backup.)

AS FOR ME, I'M still a working stiff and will likely be one until the day I die. Most of my work will probably be in the world of horror, and I have no problem with that.

After a young adulthood defined by English classical theater and insular snobbery, I've come to love horror movies and realize how important they are to the Hollywood machine, creatively, economically, and historically. But scary cinema resonates beyond the United States; the horror movie travels internationally—it's almost an ambassador, something all cultures can understand—and the genre has given me an opportunity to work around the world as a professional actor. It's opened an untold number of doors for me, and for that I'll always be thankful. If you wish to typecast me as a genre actor, so be it. Stumbling into this world was a happy accident that gave me a wonderful career.

My career has been so fulfilling and joyous that I'm not concerned about whether critics and pundits agree with me regarding horror's place in the showbiz cosmos. The chance of the Academy recognizing an out-and-out scary film is slim to none, but that's okay; I won a Lifetime Achievement Award from the Academy of Science Fiction, Fantasy, and Horror Films, and that's good enough for me.

One of my favorite Rolling Stones songs is "It's Only Rock 'n' Roll," and that's a sentiment you can apply to my world—it's only film, but I like it, like it, yes, I do. Cinema can be taken too seriously; sometimes part of the fun of going to a movie is that it's completely disposable. Most of the movies I've been a part of since *A Nightmare on Elm Street* are like celluloid comic books, enjoyable because of the immediacy of satisfaction. If there's a K-Y-jelly-covered guy in your movie wearing a claw glove and a ratty red-and-green sweater, chances are you're not going to see a piece of high art. But there's a fair to middlin' chance that you'll have a blast.

If only one of my movies survives the test of time, that's wonderful, but if I can make you forget your problems for a minute or three, I've done my job. My goal as an actor, writer, or director is that you have a great time, then you go back to your life, hopefully in a better mood, ready for a night of peaceful sleep and sweet dreams.

Or, better yet, a night of horrible sleep and brutal nightmares.

APPENDIX 1

ROBERT ENGLUND'S
MUST-SEE MOVIES

ON THE WATERFRONT

Director - Elia Kazan
Starring - Marlon Brando

One of the greatest American movies ever made. Check out the scene when Brando picks up Eva Marie Saint's glove.

THE BAND WAGON

Director - Vincente Minnelli
Starring - Fred Astaire

Terrific musical-theater spoof. The last dance number, a Mickey Spillane/Raymond Chandler detective story take-off with Cyd Charisse, is worth the price of admission by itself.

APPENDIX

ROMAN HOLIDAY

Director - William Wyler
Starring - Audrey Hepburn

Classic contemporary fairy tale. You will fall in love with Rome and Audrey Hepburn in her debut. Makes me want to go out and buy a Vespa.

EAST OF EDEN

Director - Elia Kazan
Starring - James Dean

James Dean's greatest physical performance. Check out the scene with his mother, and the stalled-merry-go-round exchange with Julie Harris.

SWEET SMELL OF SUCCESS

Director - Alexander Mackendrick
Starring - Burt Lancaster, Tony Curtis

Wonderful performances. Gritty James Wong Howe location cinematography. You'll never look at Tony Curtis the same way again.

ANATOMY OF A MURDER

Director - Otto Preminger
Starring - James Stewart

Extraordinary cast. Riveting story. Terrific courtroom scenes. Lee Remick in tight sweaters and Ray-Bans, George C. Scott's debut.

TOUCH OF EVIL

Directed by and Starring - Orson Welles

Kinky, strange, over-the-top film noir. Welles doubles fifties Venice, California, for a Mexican border town. Brilliant use of overlapping dialogue.

THE FUGITIVE KIND

Director - Sidney Lumet
Starring - Marlon Brando, Anna Magnani

Brando meets southern-Gothic Tennessee Williams again! I want his leather jacket. Watch Joanne Woodward's spoiled-rich-girl turn.

HUD

Director - Martin Ritt
Starring - Paul Newman, Patricia Neal

Newman at his best.

CHARADE

Director - Stanley Donen
Starring - Cary Grant, Audrey Hepburn

Sophisticated thriller, Paris locations, amazing supporting cast: Walter Matthau, George Kennedy, James Coburn.

APPENDIX

LORD JIM

Director - Richard Brooks
Starring - Peter O'Toole

Classic boys' adventure film. Exotic locations.

THE PROFESSIONALS

Director - Richard Brooks
Starring - Burt Lancaster, Lee Marvin

Best example of heightened "purple prose." I prefer it to *The Magnificent Seven.*

IN COLD BLOOD

Director - Richard Brooks
Starring - Scott Wilson, Robert Blake

Poetic, haunting serial-killer docudrama. Would make a good double bill with *Henry: Portrait of a Serial Killer.*

TWO FOR THE ROAD

Director - Stanley Donen
Starring - Audrey Hepburn, Albert Finney

Best dissection of a relationship on film. Funny and sad. And you get to travel the back roads of Europe in the sixties.

CHARLEY VARRICK

Director - Don Siegel
Starring - Walter Matthau

Brutal contemporary western.

MURMUR OF THE HEART
Director - Louis Malle
Starring - Lea Massari

Wise film about coming of age in a French middle-class family during the Vietnam era.

HAPPY NEW YEAR (LA BONNE ANNÉE)
Director - Claude Lelouch
Starring - Lino Ventura

One of my favorite caper films. And a philosophical one at that.

AND NOW MY LOVE (TOUTE UNE VIE)
Director - Claude Lelouch
Starring - Marthe Keller

Best use of parallel story lines I've ever seen in the cinema.

YOUNG FRANKENSTEIN
Director - Mel Brooks
Starring - Gene Wilder

My favorite comedy. Improves with age.

1900 (NOVECENTO)
Director - Bernardo Bertolucci
Starring - Robert De Niro, Gérard Depardieu

Epic film storytelling. Brilliant use of a single location as it changes with the seasons and the years. De Niro and

Depardieu in the flower of their youth. Plus Dominique Sanda. And a Grand Guignol performance by Donald Sutherland.

CLOSE ENCOUNTERS OF THE THIRD KIND
Director - Steven Spielberg
Starring - Richard Dreyfuss

Look for the slightly darker uncut version.

NIGHT OF THE SHOOTING STARS (LA NOTTE DI SAN LORENZO)
Directors - Paolo Taviani, Vittorio Taviani
Starring - Omero Antonutti

An Italian village survives Nazis at the end of World War II. An awkward shoot-out toward the end among family members and townspeople divided over the war is as startling and real as anything I've seen in the cinema. Soul-wrenching, offhand violence.

FREDDY KRUEGER'S
MUST-SEE MOVIES

20,000 LEAGUES UNDER THE SEA
Director - Richard Fleischer
Starring - Kirk Douglas, James Mason

The *Nautilus,* a giant squid, a neurotic James Mason: what else do you need? How about Kirk Douglas singing? The monster calamari's sucker wounds on the sailors ruined my summer vacation.

FORBIDDEN PLANET
Director - Fred McLeod Wilcox
Starring - Walter Pidgeon

My classmates and I argued during recess about what the "Monster of the Id" was. It took us an entire semester to figure out it was a saber-toothed tiger. (There was no video or DVD back then, remember?) We were prisoners of our imagination. A Robby the Robot action figure is on the desk next to me as I write this blurb.

THE BAD SEED

Director - Mervyn LeRoy
Starring - Patty McCormack

I accidentally saw this movie instead of a cowboy flick at a kiddie matinee birthday party. I feared the sound of tap shoes and girls with pigtails for years.

THE INNOCENTS

Director - Jack Clayton
Starring - Debra Kerr

Perfect film adaptation from a literary source. Brilliant black-and-white cinematography and sophisticated sound mix. What happened to those children? Oooh.

ROSEMARY'S BABY

Director - Roman Polanski
Starring - Mia Farrow, John Cassavetes

Perfect movie. Stands the test of time. Cassavetes's performance grows more layered each time I see it.

THE EXORCIST

Director - William Friedkin
Starring - Ellen Burstyn, Max von Sydow

Contemporary classic.

SISTERS

Director - Brian De Palma
Starring - Margot Kidder, William Finley

Best use of split screen to build suspense I've ever seen. My favorite mad doctor in the history of film.

HENRY: PORTRAIT OF A SERIAL KILLER

Director - John McNaughton
Starring - Michael Rooker

Relentless. Unnerving use of documentary style to convey claustrophobic terror.

THE DEVIL'S BACKBONE (EL ESPINAZO DEL DIABLO)

Director - Guillermo del Toro
Starring - Eduardo Noriega

Beautiful, lyric, sad ghost story with political undertones. One of the kinkiest amputee-sex scenes since *Romeo Is Bleeding*.

FRAILTY

Directed by and Starring - Bill Paxton

This film amazed me, fooled me, I never saw the ending coming. An underrated classic.

MAY

Director - Lucky McKee
Starring - Angela Bettis

Brilliant title performance, empathetic and scary at the same time. A kinky, twisted, contemporary, dysfunctional horror revenge tale set among the scruffy hills and struggling lives of East Hollywood. Don't trust your vet. Bonus, Anna Faris as a hot lesbian.

LET THE RIGHT ONE IN (LÅT DEN RÄTTE KOMMA IN)

Director - Tomas Alfredson

My favorite new take on the vampire myth. Hypnotic performances by the young leads. Forget your prejudice against subtitles and find this film!

APPENDIX 2

THE WIT AND WISDOM OF FREDDY KRUEGER

(AKA, MY TWENTY-FIVE FAVORITE FREDDY
QUOTES, IN NO PARTICULAR ORDER)

Welcome to prime time, bitch!

You're all my children now!

How sweet, fresh meat!

No screaming while the bus is in motion!

What's with kids today?

Sticks and stones may break my bones, but nothing will ever
kill me!

APPENDIX

You forgot where you came from, kid, but I know where you're going!

I've always had a thing for the whores that live in this house.

The only thing to fear is fear himself!

I should warn you, princess, the first time tends to get a little messy.

Now there's a face only your mother could love!

Your eyes say, "No, no." But my mouth says, "Yes, yes."

This is God!

Just because it's a love story doesn't mean it can't have a decapitation or two.

When you wake up, it's back in the saddle again!

I don't believe in fairy tales.

Why don't you reach out and cut someone?

You can check in, but you can't check out!

Wanna suck face?

If the food don't kill you, the service will!

You've got the body, and I've got the brain!

Kids. Always a disappointment.

Better not dream and drive.

This boy feels the need for speed!

I am eternal!

APPENDIX 3

FREDDY'S
FAVORITE KILLS

For my number-one favorite kill, I almost went with Johnny Depp being eaten alive and then regurgitated by his own bed in *A Nightmare on Elm Street*, but the winner, by a finger blade's width, has to be the death of that feisty Tina (Amanda Wyss), who put up such a fight while I thrashed her about on the ceiling of her bedroom. Freddy loves a worthy adversary, especially if it's a nubile teenaged girl.

A close second goes to my hearing-impaired victim Carlos (Ricky Dean Logan) in *Nightmare 6*. In these über–politically-correct times, it's refreshing to remember what an equal-opportunity killer Freddy always was. Not only does he pump up the volume on the hearing aid from hell, but he also adds a nice Latino kid to his body count. Today they probably wouldn't even let Freddy force-feed a fat kid junk food.

Dream death number three is found in a sequence from *Nightmare 3*. Freddy plays puppet master with victim Phillip (Bradley Gregg), converting his arm and leg tendons into marionette strings, then cutting them in a Freddy meets Vertigo moment.

The kiss of death Professor Freddy gives Sheila (Toy Newkirk) is great, but not as good as Al Pacino's in *The Godfather*, so my fourth pick is Freddy turning Debbie (Brooke Theiss) into her worst nightmare, a cockroach, and crushing her in a Roach Motel. A classic Kafka/Krueger kill.

For my final fave, you will have to check out *Freddy vs. Jason* playing at a Hell's Octoplex near you. Here's a hint: the hockey-puck guy and I double-team a member of Destiny's Child. Yummy! Now where's that Beyoncé . . .

APPENDIX 4

ROBERT ENGLUND'S
INFINITE PLAYLIST

"Naïve Medley" - Talking Heads

"Waiting in Vain" - Bob Marley and the Wailers

"(I Can't Believe) I'm Still in Love with You" - Junior Walker
    & the All Stars

"Under My Thumb" - Rolling Stones

"Stupid Girl" - Rolling Stones

"Spanish Harlem" - Aretha Franklin

"Day Dreaming" - Aretha Franklin

APPENDIX

"Gimme a Little Sign" - Brenton Wood

"Tighten Up" - Archie Bell & the Drells

"Holding Back the Years" - Simply Red

"1999" - Prince

"Come Fly with Me" - Frank Sinatra

"Come and Get These Memories" - Martha and the Vandellas

"You Beat Me to the Punch" - Mary Wells

"Spring Can Really Hang You Up the Most" - Ella Fitzgerald

"Fool in the Rain" - Led Zeppelin

"Don't Let Me Down" - The Beatles

"Lu" - Laura Nyro

"Carrie Anne" - The Hollies

"Anna (Go to Him)" - The Beatles

"Young Blood" - Rickie Lee Jones

"I Won't Grow Up" - Rickie Lee Jones

APPENDIX

"Sweet Home Alabama" - Lynyrd Skynard

"Help Me" - Joni Mitchell

"Someday, Someway" - Marshall Crenshaw

"Jaded" - Aerosmith

"Crystal Blue Persuasion" - Tommy James and the Shondells

"Game of Love" - Santana

"Walk on the Wild Side" - Lou Reed

"Like a Rolling Stone" - Bob Dylan

APPENDIX 4.5

FREDDY KRUEGER'S
BOILER ROOM MEGAMIX
FROM HELL

"Freddy Krueger" - Stormtroopers of Death

"In the Name of Freddy, Four Fingers in the Air" - F.K.Ü.
   (Freddy Krueger's Underwear)

"Four Fingers Fatal to the Flesh" - F.K.Ü.

"A Nightmare on My Street" - DJ Jazzy Jeff & the Fresh Prince

"Are You Ready for Freddy?" - The Fat Boys

"Raise Your Fist and Yell" - Alice Cooper

"Welcome to My Nightmare" - Alice Cooper

APPENDIX

"Dream Warriors" - Dokken

"In My Dreams" - Dokken

"Problem Solver" - Lil Wayne

"Haters" - Lil Wayne

"American Gangster" - Jay-Z

"I Can Be" - Eminem

"Trust" - Limp Bizkit

"Throw It Up" - Busta Rhymes

"How U Get a Record Deal?" - Big Daddy Kane

"Money" - The Game

"Dis Bitch, Dat Hoe" - Three 6 Mafia

"No Limit Soldiers" - TRU

APPENDIX 5

ROBERT ENGLUND'S SELECTED
FILM- AND VIDEOGRAPHY

1974

FILM

Buster and Billie (w/Jan-Michael Vincent and Pamela Sue Martin)

1975

FILM

Hustle (w/Burt Reynolds, Catherine Deneuve, Ben Johnson, Eileen Brennan, and Ernest Borgnine)

Slashed Dreams

1976

FILM

A Star Is Born (w/Barbra Streisand, Kris Kristofferson, and Gary Busey)

Stay Hungry (w/Jeff Bridges, Sally Field, and Arnold Schwarzenegger)

St. Ives (w/Charles Bronson, John Houseman, and Jacqueline Bisset)

1977

FILM

Eaten Alive (aka *Brutes and Savages*) (w/Neville Brand, Mel Ferrer, and Carolyn Jones)

The Last of the Cowboys (aka *The Great Smokey Roadblock*) (w/Henry Fonda, Eileen Brennan and Susan Sarandon)

TELEVISION

The Hardy Boys/Nancy Drew Mysteries (w/Shaun Cassidy, Parker Stevenson, Pamela Sue Martin, and Jamie Lee Curtis)

Young Joe, the Forgotten Kennedy (TV movie w/Peter Strauss)

1978

FILM

Big Wednesday (w/Jan-Michael Vincent, Gary Busey, and Patti D'Arbanville)

Bloodbrothers (w/Richard Gere, Paul Sorvino, and Marilu Henner)

The Fifth Floor (w/Bo Hopkins and Sharon Farrell)

TELEVISION

The Courage and the Passion (TV movie w/Desi Arnaz Jr.)

Police Woman (w/Angie Dickenson)

1979

TELEVISION

California Fever

Mind over Murder (TV movie w/Bruce Davison)

The Ordeal of Patty Hearst (TV movie w/Dennis Weaver)

Paris (w/James Earl Jones)

Soap (w/Richard Mulligan and Billy Crystal)

APPENDIX

1980

TELEVISION

Charlie's Angels (w/Jacklyn Smith, Cheryl Ladd, and Shelley Hack)

Flo

1981

FILM

Dead & Buried (w/James Farentino)

Galaxy of Terror (w/Eddie Albert, Erin Moran, Ray Walston, and Zalman King)

TELEVISION

CHiPS (w/Erik Estrada)

Hart to Hart (w/Robert Wagner and Stefanie Powers)

Walking Tall

1982

FILM

Don't Cry, It's Only Thunder (w/Dennis Christopher and Susan Saint James)

TELEVISION

Cassie & Company (w/Angie Dickinson)

Mysterious Two (TV movie w/John Forsythe)

Thou Shalt Not Kill (TV movie w/Lee Grant and Robert Culp)

1983

TELEVISION

The Fighter (TV movie w/Gregory Harrison)

Hobson's Choice (TV movie w/Lillian Gish, Jack Warden, and Richard Thomas)

I Want to Live (TV movie w/Lindsay Wagner, Harry Dean Stanton, and Martin Balsam)

Journey's End (TV movie w/George Wendt)

Manimal

Simon & Simon

Starflight: The Plane That Couldn't Land (TV movie w/Lee Majors, Hal Linden, and Lauren Hutton)

V (TV movie w/Faye Grant)

1984

FILM

A Nightmare on Elm Street (w/Heather Langenkamp, John Saxon, and Johnny Depp)

TELEVISION

Alice

V: The Final Battle (miniseries w/Faye Grant and Michael Ironside)

1985

FILM

A Nightmare on Elm Street 2: Freddy's Revenge (w/ Mark Patton and Kim Myers)

TELEVISION

Hunter (w/Fred Dryer)

Night Court (w/Harry Anderson)

V (series w/Faye Grant and Michael Ironside)

1986

FILM

Never Too Young to Die (w/John Stamos and Gene Simmons)

TELEVISION

Knight Rider (w/David Hasselhoff)

MacGyver (w/Richard Dean Anderson)

North and South, Book II (miniseries w/Kirstie Alley and David Carradine)

1987

FILM

A Nightmare on Elm Street 3: Dream Warriors (w/ Heather Langenkamp, Patricia Arquette, Laurence Fishburne, and Craig Wasson)

TELEVISION

Downtown (w/Mariska Hargitay, Blair Underwood, and Michael Nouri)

Infidelity (TV movie w/Courtney Thorne-Smith)

1988

FILM

A Nightmare on Elm Street 4: The Dream Master (w/ Tuesday Knight and Ken Sagoes)

976-EVIL (Director)

1989

FILM

C.H.U.D. II: Bud the Chud

A Nightmare on Elm Street 5: The Dream Child (w/ Lisa Wilcox and Erika Anderson)

Phantom of the Opera: The Motion Picture (w/Bill Nighy, Molly Shannon, and Jill Schoelen)

APPENDIX

1990

FILM

The Adventures of Ford Fairlaine (w/Andrew Dice Clay, Wayne Newton, Priscilla Presley, and Gilbert Gottfried)

TELEVISION

Freddy's Nightmares

1991

FILM

Freddy's Dead: The Final Nightmare (w/Lisa Zane, Shon Greenblatt, Breckin Meyer, and Johnny Depp)

1992

FILM

Dance Macabre

TELEVISION

Nightmare Café (w/Jack Coleman and Lindsay Frost)

1993

FILM

Night Terrors (w/Chandra West)

1994

FILM

New Nightmare (aka *Wes Craven's New Nightmare*) w/Heather Langenkamp, Wes Craven, John Saxon, and Bob Shaye)

TELEVISION

Mortal Fear (TV movie w/Gregory Harrison and Joanna Kerns)

A Perry Mason Mystery: The Case of the Lethal Lifestyle (TV movie w/Hal Holbrook and Dixie Carter)

1995

FILM

The Mangler (w/Ted Levine)

TELEVISION

Legend

The Unspoken Truth (TV movie w/Lea Thompson)

1996

FILM

La Lengua Asesina (w/Melinda Clarke)

The Vampyre Wars (w/Chris Sarandon, Amanda Plummer, and Maximillian Schell)

APPENDIX

TELEVISION

Babylon 5 (w/Peter Jurasik)

Sliders (w/Jerry O'Connell and John Rhys-Davies)

Walker, Texas Ranger (w/Chuck Norris)

1997

FILM

Galactic Odyssey (w/Adam Baldwin)

The Paper Brigade

Perfect Target

Wishmaster

TELEVISION

Married . . . with Children (w/Ed O'Neill, Katey Sagal, and Christina Applegate)

1998

FILM

Meet the Deedles (w/Paul Walker, Dennis Hopper, and John Ashton)

Strangeland (w/Linda Cardellini and Dee Snider)

Urban Legend (w/Jared Leto, Alicia Witt, Rebecca Gayheart, and Tara Reid)

TELEVISION

The Simpsons (w/Dan Castellaneta and Hank Azaria)

1999

FILM

The Prince and the Surfer

TELEVISION

The Hughleys (w/D. L. Hughley)

The Jamie Foxx Show (w/Jamie Foxx)

2000

FILM

Python (TV movie w/Wil Wheaton and Jenny McCarthy)

2001

TELEVISION

Charmed (w/Alyssa Milano and Rose McGowan)

The Nightmare Room

FILM

Windfall (TV movie w/Casper Van Dien and Ray Wise)

2002

FILM

As a Bad Dream

Cold Sweat (w/Melinda Clarke)

Nobody Knows Anything (w/Janeane Garofalo and Margaret Cho)

Il Ritorno di Cagliostro

Wish You Were Dead (w/Cary Elwes, Christopher Lloyd, Mary Steenburgen, and Billy Ray Cyrus)

2003

TELEVISION

I'm With Her (w/Teri Polo)

2004

FILM

Dubbed and Dangerous 3

Freddy vs. Jason (w/Kelly Rowland, Monica Keena, and Jason Ritter)

TELEVISION

Super Robot Monkey Team Hyperforce Go!

2005

FILM

2001 Maniacs (w/Peter Stormare)

TELEVISION

Justice League

Masters of Horror (Showtime)

2006

FILM

Behind the Mask: The Rise of Leslie Vernon

Hatchet

Heartstopper

2007

FILM

Jack Brooks: Monster Slayer

TELEVISION

The Batman

Black Swarm (Sci Fi Channel)

Bodog Music Battle of the Bands

APPENDIX

2008

FILM

Red (w/Brian Cox and Tom Sizemore)

Killer Pad (Director)

Zombie Strippers! (w/Jenna Jameson)

TELEVISION

The Spectacular Spider-Man

2009

FILM

Night of the Sinner

ACKNOWLEDGMENTS

I could probably spend this entire book recalling nuances from the run of one play or the adventures of a single film location. But economy and my desire to give an affectionate survey of my fortunate career prevents that attention to detail. If, after some six decades, recollections and secondhand stories have faded, blended, or lost their proper chronology, I apologize to all participants for any flawed reporting. It's been a long haul. Regarding the sin of omission, I beg forgiveness of any friends or coworkers who feel slighted by exclusion: surfing buddies, drinking companions, lovers, FX makeup teams, prop crews, costars, and film editors who saved my sorry ass—you know who you are and how much you have meant to me.

For words of early encouragement, advice, career direction, and teaching: Jean Klenes, Deane Wolfson, Steve Allen, Janice Farquar, James Rawley, Jeff Corey, Paul Lee, Joseph Shaw, John Fernald, and Lawrence Carra.

For professional guidance, past and present, thank you, Lew Sherrell and Jo Martin, who put up with me during the seventies; Joseph E. Rice, who has returned my calls and been my

ACKNOWLEDGMENTS

good friend and agent since 1982; Wayne Rice, whose artistic savvy and foresight as the architect of my finances has given me the freedom to live for the past twenty years in my little bungalow by the sea with my best girl and my old dogs by my side and the happy ghosts of my parents looking on; and Stephen Lo, for all those airline upgrades. And to Harry Abrams, whose letterhead gives this old whore a touch of class.

To friends old and new, Gary Tigerman, Doug Matheson, Russ Laxson, Steve Smith, Terry Judge, Hugh Corcoran, David Himes, Bruce Gray, Jonathan Benair, Chris Buchinsky, Rick Dano, Anthony Friedkin, David Irving, Don Bajema, Bob Lepucki, Jane Handel, Loris Curci, and my best buddy, Demetre Phillips.

A heartfelt thank-you to Wes Craven and Tobe Hooper for taking the time to write those kind words, and for hiring me time and again. And thanks to Carly Feingold for her help in wrangling Wes.

Thanks to everybody at Pocket Books, especially my editor Jaime Costas, VP and Deputy Publisher Anthony Ziccardi, and Publisher Louise Burke, as well as to Jarred Weisfeld and the gang at Objective Entertainment.

A special thanks to my collaborator, Alan Goldsher, who managed to somehow quickly and accurately assimilate a zillion stories into a cool little book that I'll always be proud of.

And finally, much love to my beautiful wife, Nancy, without whom none of this matters. You're the woman of my dreams.

Printed in the United States
By Bookmasters